Bondag
&
The Straw Chair

Bondagers
'One of the finest plays of the modern Scottish theatre . . . it is raw and rough, warm and tender, funny enough to make your heart dance and moving enough to steal it away . . . This is a play that everyone should see' *Scotland on Sunday*

'A striking experience . . . rich, resonant musicality . . . And did that language roll; it swept in great waves of earthy sound. All brilliantly structured, surging – with terrific dramatic energy' *Glasgow Herald*

The Straw Chair
'The dialogue is crisp and telling and has no truck with the whimsy and feyness which so often bedevils Scots writing about the past' *The Times*

'A beguiling combination of things, starting with the incredible story of Lady Grange, banished by her husband to the remoteness of St Kilda. Hung around this framework is an evocation, as light and sharp as spindrift, of the strange life on the island' *Scotland on Sunday*

Sue Glover was born in Edinburgh and lives in North-east Fife. She writes for radio, television and theatre. Theatre work includes *The Seal Wife, The Bubble Boy, The Straw Chair* and *Sacred Hearts. The Bubble Boy* was staged during Glasgow Tron Theatre's opening season, and later televised, winning prizes at both the New York Film and Television Festival and the Chicago International Festival. *The Straw Chair* opened the Traverse Theatre's 25th Anniversary season. *Bondagers* won first prize in London Weekend Television's Plays on Stage Awards in 1990. At present Sue Glover is working on a commission for the Royal National Theatre Studio (working title, *Kinder*), and a film about artists and models, set in Glasgow at the turn of the century.

Methuen Modern Plays also available

Claire Dowie
Why Is John Lennon Wearing A Skirt? and other stand-up
theatre plays

David Greig
Europe & The Architect

Jonathan Harvey
Boom Bang-A-Bang & Rupert Street Lonely Hearts Club

Phyllis Nagy
Weldon Rising & Disappeared

Joe Penhall
Some Voices & Pale Horse

Stephen Poliakoff
Sweet Panic & Blinded by the Sun

Shelagh Stephenson
The Memory of Water & Five Kinds of Silence

Judy Upton
Bruises & The Shorewatchers' House

Sue Glover

Bondagers
&
The Straw Chair

Methuen Drama

Methuen Publishing Ltd.,
11–12 Buckingham Gate, London SW1E 6LB

First published in Great Britain 1997
by Methuen Drama

Reprinted 2005

Bondagers first published by Methuen Drama in 2005
Made in Scotland Copyright © 1995 by Sue Glover
The Straw Chair Copyright © 1997 by Sue Glover
The author has asserted her moral rights

ISBN 0 413 71210 9

A CIP catalogue record for this book is available from the
British Library

Typeset by 10.5 on 11.5 point Baskerville by
Wilmaset, Birkenhead, Wirral
Printed and bound in Great Britain by Cox & Wyman Ltd,
Reading Berkshire

Contents

Bondagers

For Muriel Romanes, who told me about the bondagers

Bondagers was first performed in May 1991 at The Tramway, Glasgow, and at the Traverse Theatre, Edinburgh. The cast was as follows:

Liza	Hilary Maclean
Maggie	Anne Lacey
Sara	Ann Louise Ross
Tottie	Myra MacFadyen
Ellen	Rosaleen Pelan
Jenny	Eve Keepax

Directed by Ian Brown
Designed by Steward Laing
Lighting by Paule Constable
Movement by Sue MacLennan
Music by Pete Livingstone
Dialect coach Ros Steen

The production was revived at the new Traverse Theatre in November in 1993 and later toured Canada. The cast remained the same, except that Kathryn Howden played Tottie and in Canada Carole Ann Crawford played Maggie. When the production was revived a third time in 1995, playing in Edinburgh, London, Canada and Budapest, Julie Duncanson played Jenny.

Setting

Bondagers were the women workers of the great Border farms in the last century. Each farm worker was hired on condition he brought a female worker to work alongside hin – if not his wife or daughter, then some other girl that he himself had to hire at the Hiring Fair, and lodge and feed alongside his own family in his tiny cottage.

The play is set on a Border farm of 1860. Act One – with the exception of the opening scene (the 'Hiring') – takes place in summer; Act Two in winter. The set should be minimal. One area of the acting space should represent Maggie's house – but not so definitely as to be intrusive when it does not figure in the action. The cradle is in this 'area' – it is a statement, and should be visible. Possibly an 'area' of the acting space represents Sara's house (when required – again, not intrusively). But the 'house' area(s) should simply be used as part of the field, barn, whatever, during other scenes; all areas can 'come and go', as it were.

The bondagers' dress was distinctive and unique: almost a uniform. Something approximating it is necessary: boots or clogs; full skirts with two or three petticoats; 'headhankies' – i.e. kerchiefs that covered their heads, and were, when work and weather required, tied over the chin, or even the whole lower part of the face. But the bondagers' most notable trademark, worn over the headhankie, was the black straw bonnet: trimmed with red ruching, and lined with the same sprigged cotton that they used for their blouses. Muddy, sometimes shabby, but beguiling.

The bondagers used a sickle that the ancient Egyptians would have recognised. More agricultural advances have been made in the last 200 years than in the last eight thousand. But periods of plenty and progress are relentlessly interrupted by leaner, harsher times: bad weather, bad harvests, bad government, disease ... and the sometimes unfortunate, sometimes devastating, consequences of our innovations and discoveries. And so the ghosts in the field come and go. Tottie sees this; she stands for the land. And Kello stands for our (sometimes criminal) carelessness.

Act One

Scene One

Liza, **Sara**, **Jenny**, **Tottie** *in the market place, for the Hiring Fair.* **Maggie** *at home.*

Voices (*all the cast, cutting in on each other's phrases, some of the phrases can be repeated. Low whispers at first, growing louder*)
The Hiring, the Hiring, the Hiring . . .
Hiring Fair, Hiring Fair, Hiring Fair . . .
What a folk/What a crowd/What a carts/What a people/
What a noise!
Ye get a' the clash at the Hiring.
Ye get a' the fun at the Fair.
I'm blythe to see ye
Tam/Andra/Jenny/Meg/William/Neil/Geordie/Joe/Jane/
Jack.
What fettle? Fine fettle. How's the cow? Doing grand. How's
a' wi you? How's the bairns . . . and the cow? How's the wife
. . . and the cow?
Did you ken about Davie/Jockie/Tam/Sandy/Nathan/Ned/
Mary/Betsy/Bob?
What's the crack?/Heard the crack from Langriggs/
Redriggs/Smiddyhill/Smiddyford/Horsecleugh/
Oxencleugh/Whitehas/Blacksheils/East Mains/Westlea.

During this **Liza** *is wandering, jostled by the crowd, looking for a place to stand.*

Voices (*these phrases more distinct*)
The Hiring, the Hiring Fair.
First Monday in February.
Coldest Monday in February.
Eight o'clock. Soon as it's licht.
See the farmers bargain wi the hinds.
See the hinds bargain wi the bondagers.
See the bonny bondagers stand in a row.

Liza *has chosen her place, waits to be hired.* **Sara** *and* **Tottie** *are also standing now together, waiting to be hired.*

First voice (*low whisper*)   The coldest Monday. Soon as it's licht. (*Louder, taunting.*) No bondager worth a puckle's left after ten o clock.

Liza (*outwardly defiant – not in answer to the voice, and never speaking directly to the audience*)   I'll be gone long afore ten. Bound over. Hired. See if I'm not. Broad shoothers, short back, strong legs.

Sara   Stand here Tottie, stand still now.

Liza
– I'll not take the arle from the first that comes,
I'm only going to a well-kent hind.
I can shear come harvest. I'm good with the horses.
I'll fettle the horses – but not your bairns.
I'll redd up the steading – but not your house,
I'll work a' day – but not in your bed.

Sara   Tut, lass, dinna talk that way.

Liza
– Broad shoothers, short back, strong legs.
The good name of Tam Kerr, deceased, to live up to,
And my brother Steenie, over the seas.

Jenny   No bondager worth a puckle's left after ten o clock.

Liza   I'll be hired by ten of the clock . . . I'll take the arle by ten of the clock.

Sara   Stand straight, Tottie, dinna look sweer.

Jenny   No cottar wife's hired till the back o twelve. *Gin* she's hired.

Sara (*to* **Tottie**)   Look sonsie, can't you?

Tottie   I'm hungry.

Sara   Maybe we'll buy a tuppenny loaf after?

Tottie   After what?

Sara   After we're hired.

Jenny   *Gin* she's hired!

Tottie   There's the Maister o Langriggs – maybe we'll get to Langriggs.

Sara   Maybe. Look sonsie, now.

Voices (*each line spoken singly, in turn, by the cast*)
Ten bolls of oatmeal
Fifteen bushels barley
Six bushels pease
Twelve hundred yards potatoes, planted
A peck of lint, sown
Three pounds sheep siller
Grass for the cow
The privilege of keeping hens
Four carts of coals

First voice   It is customary to give them their meat during one month of harvest. They may keep a pig. Their wives must shear in harvest. The hinds are also bound to hire and keep a field worker, a female servant called a bondager, commonly paid ten pence a day. (. . .) The hinds complain of this; the wives even more so.

Maggie (*at home. Very busy. Washing clothes, churning butter – or knitting – she knits on the hoof, whilst she's watching a porridge pot, or rocking the cradle. Not directly to audience*)   Coldest Monday since Hallowe'en. I should have put straw in his shoon. He's well respected, my man Andra. Any farmer would be thankful to hire him. He was up afore dawn to be there for the Hiring. Kirk claes. Kirk shoon. And a shave like he hasnae had since the kirn. Three things a hind depends on: a good wife, a good cow – and a good razor.

First voice   A good hind needs a good maister.

Maggie   He can take his pick o maisters.

First voice   A good hind needs a good bondager.

Maggie   He can take his pick o bondagers . . . gin he knows how. But some o those lassies wear two faces – one for the hiring, and another for the farm! Just so long as the lass can shear – I can't work harvest, not with the bairns. Just so long as she takes to the bairns!

Liza   I'm not going to any place hoatchin wi bairns!

Sara (*to* **Liza**)   Tuts, lassie – there's bound to be bairns!

Maggie   See and pick right, Andra. Pick a good maister! Dinna say yes to the first farmer that slaps your hand and offers a dram. There's questions to be asked! Two rooms! I'd like a house with two rooms. The maister at Langriggs bigged a new row of houses – all with the two rooms . . .

Sara   We don't hope for much, Tottie and me. Day and way.

Liza   I want a place on a big farm. Plenty lassies for the crack. Plenty plooman for the dancing!

Maggie   A house near the pump. A roof without holes.

Sara (*coming in on* **Maggie**'s *line*)   A roof without holes.

Sarah *and* **Maggie**   Good pasture for the cow.

Sara   Kindness for Tottie – she's slow – she has days.

Tottie   Bad days! Bad days!

Liza   No bairns underfoot.

Maggie   And if it's a good place – maybe we'll stay – not just the year . . . longer. Same house, same farm, same kirk, same neighbours . . . (*Realising it's an unlikely notion.*) Aye! Well! – so long as it's dry for the flitting.

Sara (*coming in on her last line*)   So long as it's dry for the flitting.

Tottie   I doubt it'll rain for the flitting, Mammy!

Liza   I'll buy a new hat for the flitting.

Scene Two

Liza, Tottie, Ellen. Liza *walking away from the fair,* **Tottie** *comes after her.*

Tottie (*to* **Liza**)   You, you, you. What farm are you going to? What farm?

Liza *not answering, doesn't think much of* **Tottie**. **Tottie** *insistent*.

What farm?

Liza   Blacksheils.

Tottie   So are we. Which hind will ye work with?

Liza   Andra Innes.

Tottie   We're on our own. Mammy and me. (*Trying to keep* **Liza***'s attention*.) There's ghosts at Blacksheils. Up on the moor.

Liza (*not impressed by ghosts*)   Is it still Maister Elliott farms Blacksheils?

Tottie   The one that married Ellen. Ellen Rippeth that was. She worked with us at Blacksheils. Not last year. Before. Before she set her cap at the maister.

Liza   I know.

Tottie   *You* weren't there.

Liza   I was at Billieslaw. Over the hill. I was bondager to my brother.

Tottie   Set her cap at him, and married him and a'. That's how we got hired. For the sake o lang syne.

Liza   Ellen Rippeth never gave any favours.

Tottie   Ay, she does. She's the mistress now.

Ellen (*practising using a fan, elegantly, expertly*)   Learn to use a fan? I can single turnips in the sweat; shaw them in the sleet – I can surely use a fan! Take tea with the gentry? They talk about turnips. Yield, rotation, manure. They know about turnips. Their shoes are shiny, clothes clean, shoothers dry. We were soaked to the skin by half past eight, in the mist, in the morning. Frost, snow, sun, wind, rain; single, shaw, howk, mangle, cart. Aye. We kenned about neeps!

Scene Three

Liza *and* **Maggie**. **Maggie** *is busy, very.* (*The baby and the porridge pot both at once.*) **Liza** *arrives with her bundle of worldly goods.*

Liza   I'm Liza. The bondager.

Maggie   I'm Maggie, his wife. You'll have seen the bairns, they're playing round the doors.

Liza   Which are yours?

Maggie   All of them, nearly.

Liza   The wee laddie that kicks?

Maggie (*serene*)   Kicks? Oh, no, never – you must have got in the way. My bairns wouldna kick. Now. Then. (*Proudly.*) We've the two box beds. So you can share the other one with the bairns.

Liza   I'll not. I'll not sleep with bairns. I'll sleep in the roof.

Maggie (*serene*)   The older bairns sleep in the roof.

Liza   A couple of bairns, he said, at the Hiring!

Maggie (*serene*)   Andra said that? No, no – you'll have got it wrong. Andra would never deny his ain bairns! You were gabbing to some other hind, nae doubt! Here – see to the pot while I see to the babby. (*She is busy with the baby.*) Liza Kerr? Steenie Kerr's sister? There were only the two of you after Tam crossed the Jordan. And a whole house to yourselves? But lassie – naebody round here has a bed to hisself! I dinna ken anyone that sleeps alone – save the plooman up in the steading – mind you, from what I hear, there's one of the dairymaids – still, it's early days yet to pass judgement. You'll soon love the bairns. You're a lassie, after all – you're bound to love them. (*Sharp appraisal.*) Can you shear?

Liza   Aye.

Maggie   You'll do!

Scene Four

All of them, except **Ellen**. *They are singling turnips. In their large
hats and headhankies tied over their chins, they are not individually
recognisable. The five of them are part of a larger squad, the 'field'
onstage is part of an enormous field – thirty or forty acres. They work
fast, each moving along her own drill, keeping more or less in pace with
the others. (***Tottie*** *is slower, maybe much slower.) The dialogue,
when it comes, is fast, fragmented, overlapping. It comes in spurts,
with pauses between. And they never stop working. Obviously the gist
of the dialogue is important, equally, though, every phrase does not have
to be heard. The only lines that have to be spoken by particular
characters are* **Jenny**'*s and* **Liza**'*s.*

(*Two of them sing.*)
Woo'd and married and a'
Kissed and carried awa
And is no the bride well off
That's woo'd and married and a'

I'd bind more rags round your hands, if I were you lass!

I've nane.

Straw, then. Rope. We'll have to mak mair.

The saddler's come! That's him just passed the gate!

Aw, now, there's a bonny callant!

He'll no be staying more than a week!

That's what makes him bonny!

I'll get a bit crack with him when I redd up the stables!

I'll redd up the stables.

No, you'll no!

Saddler's mine!

Laughter. Pause.

Is he married, the saddler?

No.

Can he dance?

Can he dance!

Fiddle and dance all at once – as good as yon dancing maister frae Jeddart!

We'll hae a bit dance, then!

I'll hae a bit dearie!

Laughter.

Ye're an awful lassie, Jenny!

A'body wants the saddler!

A'body want a bit dearie!

(*Singing*.)   Woo'd and married and a'
Kissed and carried awa
Was she nae very well off
Was woo'd and married an a'

Was Sara married?

Dinna ken. Was Sara married?

Dinna ken.

She was going to marry Wabster, my mother said.

She was never married.

She was never neglected.

Jenny *and* **Liza** *together*:

Jenny Can ye spin, Liza – ye get to work up at the Big House if ye can spin.

Liza Don't want to spin.

Jenny It's good work on a rainy day. Better than being laid off. And you get your meat, sitting down in the kitchen.

Liza I can't spin.

Ye ken yon plooman with the curls?

Kello?

By, he can dance! Tappity with his clogs – and a kind of singsong he makes all the while – right there in the glaur, at the tweak o a bonnet.

Is he a Gyptian?

Dinna ken. His eyes are black!

Of course he's a Gyptian!

A mugger!

A tinkler!

Maister Elliott hiring Gyptians!

The maister's brown as a peatbog himself!

Maister's a gentleman!

Married one of us, though!

He's still a gentleman!

Maybe the other gentry don't think so!

Nellie makes a braw lady!

Aye – the besom!

Mistress Ellen.

Mistress *Elliott*!

Was she no very well off
Was woo'd and married an a'

(*Shouts coming from the far end of the field.*) Ye can stop now, stop at the end of the drill. We're stopping – Jenny! Liza!

They rest on their hoes, flex their backs, leave the field. **Jenny** *and* **Liza**, *slightly apart from the others. Stop to talk.*

Jenny   You're lucky biding with Maggie. She keeps a good kitchen.

Liza   I'm aye starving all the same. And I sleep with the bairns.

Jenny   So do I – I'm glad of the bairns!

Liza   Could you not sleep in the roof?

Jenny And have him creeping all over me?

Liza Who?

Jenny Who! Who do you think? (*As* **Liza** *gapes, astonished.*) Close your gob, Liza, the flies'll get in!

Liza But – his wife?

Jenny It's his bairns keep me safe, not his wife. I can teach ye to spin, Liza. If you're wanting work up at the Big House.

Liza (*suddenly irritable*) I'm not wanting work at the house.

Jenny Oh, well –! (*Walking off, then stops to call back at* **Liza**.) Besom you!

Scene Five

Liza *and* **Tottie**. **Liza** *on her own. She slumps, tired, leaning against or sitting on something, starts unwinding the rags that were bound round her hands.* **Tottie** *comes on; stands and stares at her.* **Liza** *still uncertain of* **Tottie**.

Liza Go away! Shoo!

This has no effect. Tries a frightening face or gesture.

Aaaaaargh!

Tottie *for a moment impassive, then, grinning, copies her.*

Tottie Aaaaaaargh! (*Gives* **Liza** *a shove.*) Maggie says to come and mind the babby for it's girny and she has to milk the coo.

Liza If it's girny, it's wet, if it's wet it's likely mingin'. (*Sweetly.*) You mind the babby, Tottie. Go on. Go and sing to bee-baa-babbity.

Tottie Don't you like babbies? You're a motherless bairn. *And* a fartherless bairn. And you've no brother either, for he's gone to Canada.

Liza *tries to ignore her. She lies or slumps, wanting to rest, pulling her headhankie right up and forward, hiding her face.*

Tottie My daddy's gone to Canada. My daddy's been away for a hundred year. (*The word is a talisman for her.*) Sas-katch-e-wan. Sas-katch-e-wan. (*A silence.*) There's dancing tonight.

Liza Where?

Tottie In the turnip shed. The saddler's fetching his fiddle. Maybe ye'll hae a bit dearie.

Liza What's that supposed to mean?

Tottie That's what Jenny always says. 'A'body needs a bit dearie.'

Liza Away and see to the babbity!

Liza *walks away.*

Tottie Where are you going?

Liza To the pump. To wash off the glaur!

Tottie *goes over to the cradle.*

Tottie Bee-baa-babbity. Are ye wet? Ugh! Are ye mingin'? UUUUgh! (*Hastily, in case she sets it howling.*) Don't cry, don't cry. (*Very matter-of-fact, as if to someone much older.*) I'll tell you a story. I'll tell you about the ghostie. It's true. I was up on the moors. The maister sent me. With a message for the herd. And the mist came doon – and roon – and doon. I was feared. And I shouted for the herd. But the mist smoored my words. And then I heard, very close: 'Shoough . . . shooough . . . shooough . . . ' – a plough shoughin through the ground, and whiles whanging a stane or twa. And a man, calling to his beasts: 'Coooooop, coooooop'. Like a crow. I could feel the beasts on the ground, I could feel them through my feet. Oxen. I could smell them. I wanted to walk with the plooman till the mist parted. I shouted. But the mist swirled roon and smoored a'thing. After, Jock the herd said: (*She copies his patronising tone.*) 'Naebody ploughs there, Tottie – the only rigs there are the lang syne rigs. Ye can see the marks still. Hundreds of year old. But ye'll no see ony plooman, and ye'll no see ony plough.' Aye. But I heard him though . . .

Voices (*low whispery*)
Lang syne ploughman
Lang syne rigs, rigs, rigs, rigs
Lang syne barley, barley, barley, barley
Barley means bread, oats means bread, pease means bread
Bread of carefulness
Never enough bread

Children's voices (*or the cast on stage as children; loud, matter-of-fact, unkind*)
Tottie's seen a bogle, Tottie's seen a ghostie.
Tottie's a softie, Tottie's a daftie.

Tottie (*cutting into these lines*)   I'm not. Stop it. I'm not.

First child   Sixpence in the shilling

Tottie   Stop it! No!

Second child   No all there.

Tottie   I am! (*Upset, blundering about, wanting to shove, shout down her tormentors.*)

Children (*jeering, laughing*)
Your mammy lay with Wabster
Gat ye in the cornrigs
Cleckit in the barley rigs
Coupled
Covered
Ploughed

Tottie   Married! (*Upset, aggressive – she has blundered into or pushed the cradle, it's rocking wildly.*)

First child   In the cornrigs?

Tottie   Yes.

Second child   In the *cornrigs*?

Tottie   Yes. Yes. She had a babby. It was me.

First child (*soft, sly*)   And where's your daddy now?

Tottie (*whisper*)   Sas-katch-e-wan ... Sas-katch-e-wan.

She goes to the cradle, blundering, whimpering. She has to steady the cradle, and in doing so quietens herself.

Scene Six

Sara, **Tottie**, **Ellen**, **Liza**. **Tottie** *is maybe still by the cradle.* **Sara** *busy cleaning horse tack, or patching/sewing sacks, or winding the home-made straw rope into neat oval balls: any wet-weather work.* **Ellen** *— adjusting, admiring her clothes, hat? umbrella? — half pleased at her elevated status, but half laughing at herself.*

Ellen   Sweet wheaten bread, and tea, and cream and sugar and ham! All this for breakfast! Brought by a servant girl better dressed than I ever was till now. A table like snow, a floor like a looking-glass; china, lace. Great wide windows to let in the sun – to look out on the fields. Every field fifty acres square. Hedges trim. No weeds. No waste.

Tottie *stares at her, delighted to see her. Admires and is fascinated by* **Ellen**. **Ellen** *has always tolerated* **Tottie**, *with an offhand but genuine acceptance.*

I saw you hoeing the fields this morning. I watched till you left off because of the rain.

Tottie   We don't know what to call you now.

Sara   We must call her Mistress Elliott now.

Ellen   Aye. That's what you cry me.

Seeing **Tottie**'s *grinning welcome,* **Ellen** *goes to her, hugs her.* **Tottie**'s *reciprocating hug is uninhibited, wholehearted.*

Sara *(fearful of* **Ellen**'s *gown)*   Mind now, Tottie.

Ellen   I wear this one to take tea.

Sara   There's no tea here, Nell!

Ellen   I have just taken tea – at Langriggs.

An awkwardness. She sits down very carefully. **Tottie** *gapes at her happily.* **Sarah** *motions to* **Tottie** *to start work.*

Tottie (*still with her eyes on* **Ellen**)   Ellen Rippeth-that-was.
Like a lady now. She sits like a lady.

Ellen   It's the stays. Can't bend forrard. Can't bend back.
I'm tied up every morning – let loose at bedtime.

Tottie   Who ties you – the maister?

Ellen (*to* **Sara**)   D'you mind Betty Hope? The maister's
auld mither hired her for my maid.

Sara   She's got the sort of face that comes in useful for a
wake.

Ellen   Nae crack from Betsy. It's hot in here.

Tottie   It's wet out there!

Sara   Too wet for work. The lassies are throwing their
money at the packman. The lads are in the stables, larking.

Tottie   Larking!

Ellen   By, it rained for the flitting. I watched the carts from
the window, coming down the loan. Bung fu': beds, bairns,
clocks, dressers, grandpas, geraniums – a'thing drookit.

Sara   I've a hundred rheumatisms since the flitting.
Maggie's bairns have the hoast yet.

Ellen   My shoothers are always dry now. If my stockings
are soaked, or my shoes, someone fetches another pair.

Sara   'And was she no very well off – /That's woo'd and
married an a'!'

Ellen   Here, Tottie – let loose my stays! (*Shows* **Tottie** *where
to loosen the laces under the bodice.*)

Sara (*shaking her head at* **Nell**'*s old ways*)   Mistress Elliott!

Ellen *flops on the straw.* **Tottie** *imitates her.* **Sara** *never stops
working.*

Tottie   Bad Nell!

Ellen   Not now! I'm a married lady now!

Tottie   Are you having a baby? Is it in there yet?

Ellen   No ... Not yet.

Sara (*after a pause; softly*)   There's time enough.

Ellen   A hind wouldn't think so! Some of them would have you swelled before they called the banns, even!

Sara   Och, now, Ellen –

Ellen   Well, it's true!

Sara   Not at Blacksheils. The maister wouldn't stand for it. He's stricter than the minister.

Ellen   He's – he's – a fine man. Keeps his passion under hidlings, though!

Sara   And his mother, the widow?

Ellen   She calls me 'the new blood'. 'No sense growing prize turnips, Gordon, without prize sons to mind them!'

Sara   Well, you know what they say: the bull is half the herd.

Ellen *lolls in the hay. More like the bondager she used to be.*

Ellen   Is that true for folk, as well as beasts?

Sara   Must be. Surely.

Ellen   He had a son. It died before it got born. It killed its mother before it was even born.

Tottie   How could a baby kill you?

Sara   The Elliotts have farmed here since I don't know when. His grandfather drained those cold fields of clay. He died before they were ever first cropped. Look at them now. Tatties, clover, the finest neeps in Europe. People come from all over – Germany, England – just to look at Blacksheils, and talk with the maister.

Ellen   A son for Blacksheils. Of course he wants a son.

Tottie (*tormenting* **Ellen**, *pulling at her*)   How could a bull be half the herd? How could a baby kill you?

Ellen Babies are mischief. Like you, Tottie! No telling what they'll do.

Liza *appears*.

Sara It's Liza, Mistress Elliott. Liza Kerr. Andra's bondager.

Tottie (*to* **Liza**) You must cry her Mistress Elliott, now.

Liza *gives a bob*.

Ellen (*getting up, brushing off the straw — but not put out at being caught lolling there by a servant*) I would hardly have known you. You've grown.

Ellen *is going*.

Liza Steenie's in Canada.

Ellen Yes, I heard. I hope he's well?

Liza *doesn't answer*. **Ellen** *goes*.

Liza (*muttering after her*) No thanks to you if he's well. No thanks to you!

Tottie (*softly*) Sas-katch-e-wan.

Liza Steik yer gab, you!

Gives **Tottie** *a shove, as she goes*.

Tottie Sas-katch-e-wan.

Scene Seven

Ellen, Maggie, Sara. *They are not 'together', but in their separate areas*.

Ellen Steenie Kerr. He was only a bairn. Lovesick loon! Heart on his sleeve. Scratching my name on the steading walls.

Sara Poor Steenie. I felt heart-sorry for him.

Ellen He played on pity. Punished me with other folk's pity. Used me.

Maggie   She led him a dance.

Sara   Well, he wouldn't take no.

Maggie   She drove them a' wild, the plooman.

Sara   Such a beautiful summer.

Maggie   Not for Steenie.

Sara   They were a' mad for dancing – danced every night. Till the first field was cut. And the night of the kirn – the moon was so bonny, a real harvest moon.

Ellen   I was angry. I'll show you, I thought. Steenie, all of you. I felt angry. Wild. The maister was there in the fields every day, keeping an eye on things. In the fields. At the kirn . . . Ye'll hae a dance, maister? . . . Anither dance, maister? . . . And ye'll hae a bit mair dance, maister . . . He looked that – modest! He made me laugh. He made me want. Stricter than the minister, a'body said. I'll have him in the hay, efter, I thought. Why not? A'body needs a bit dearie. And then I thought – never mind the hay, Nell – ye can mak it tae the bed. Ye can mak the Big Hoose. Ye'll can cry the banns. I could see it in his eyes. Feel it in his bones. (. . .) He cried out when he loved me. Not blubbing like Steenie, not like I wasn't there at the end, but like he was wanting to take me with him . . . Just a bit dearie. And what do I get? A'thing. I got a'thing.

Scene Eight

Maggie, Sara, Liza, Jenny.

Maggie   Did you hear about Marjie Brockie? Buckled up wi Jamie Moodie! Buckled up at Coldstream Brig. Ca' that a wedding?

Sara   It's legal.

Maggie   The minister wouldn't say so. Folk should marry in kirk with the full connivance of the Almighty. A lad and lass walk into the inn, and someone says 'Who's the lass, then?' and the lad says 'O, she's my wife!'! Ca' that a wedding?

Sara   Well, it's legal!

Maggie   It's a scandal!

Sara   It's cheaper that way. Kirk weddings cost. No wonder they run off to Coldstream under hidlings. After the fair. Or after the kirn.

Liza   Did you run away to Coldstream?

Sara   No, Liza. We were handfasted, Patie and me. We lived together, man and wife, for nearly a year, to see how we would do.

Maggie   Handfasting! And who's left holding the bairn?

Sara   But that's what they're waiting for, often as not, to see if there's a bairn. It's the baby leads them to the kirk, eventually.

Maggie   Or sends the man fleeing. To Canada, for instance.

Sara   Patie loved the baby. She was a queer bit babby, wheezy and choky. He knew she wasn't quite natural. But he loved her, you mustn't think he didn't, she was ours. He was restless, though. He wanted – something, adventure, Canada. It was me said no, I wouldn't go. This parish was my calf-ground: Langriggs, Blackshiels, Billieslaw; the fields, the river, the moor up yonder with the lang syne rigs. Patie loved the land. 'Her'. But maybe I loved her more. When it came to the bit. When it came to Greenock – and even there the land seemed foreign. And the sea; and the ships. A sad, sad place. A great crush of folk, all quiet, and a highland lass singing. Then a voice cried out, loud: 'Hands up for Canada! Hands up for Canada!' A rushing, like wings, all the hands held high. And the baby screamed like she'd never grat before. Such a stab in my heart it made the milk spurt from me. I couldn't step forward. I couldn't go on. And Patie couldn't stay. I knew he couldn't stay. He crossed the ocean;

I looked for the carter to take us back home. Patie Wabster. I think of him every day, many times every day.

Maggie Fourteen years! He'll have bairns of his own now.

Sara I hope so surely. He was made for happiness, Patie.

Liza and **Jenny** are all ears, gripped by all this.

Maggie Well! (*She hasn't heard so much of this story before, is shocked, disapproving, of* **Sara**.) Well, you've made your bed, you must lie on it.

Sara (*laughs easily*) I've no leisure for my bed!

Maggie As ye sow, shall ye reap! A cottar wife's bound to be hard-wrought!

Sara (*serenely*) Day and way!

Maggie (*annoyed, and shows it in the way she is working, with thumps and bangs – feels* **Sara** *should be regretful and guilty about this*) Well, it takes all sorts! . . . There's naught so queer as folk! . . . (*Exasperation.*) A kirk wedding would have bound you both! . . . (*More to* **Liza** *now.*) You have to bring them to account. Andra wouldn't ask me. He *wouldn't*. He was never going to ask. So when he was standing with a crowd of lads, I flew to his neck and measured him for the sark. His wedding sark.

Liza and **Jenny** start to giggle at this.

Maggie Once word got round I was sewing him the sark, well, he had no choice, he had to call the banns. And not before time.

Maggie *either goes offstage, busy on some errand, or busies herself with some work; has left* **Sara** *and* **Liza** *on their own.*

Sara (*to* **Liza** *and* **Jenny**) She doesn't understand. And neither do you, I daresay. And neither did I, at the time. Patie was lovely, like no one else. Happy, clever. But he needed to wander, he wanted the world. I have to bide still, I have to stay where I am.

Jenny But you don't bide still – you flit every year!

Sara (*laughs*)   Aye, so I do! But I never flit far. I've never been further than the three, four farms; never been further than – oh – twenty miles, maybe.

Liza   But you went as far as Greenock once.

An assent from **Sara***.*

I could go to Canada.

Sara   Well, you could. And join your brother.

Liza   Saskatchewan. I could go there. Is it a big place?

Sara   It's a place I think about every day. But I don't know what it's like. I wonder: do they have peewees? Patie loved the peewees, he'd never plough a peewee's nest, he'd steer the horses round it. We understood each other. Tottie's part of that, part of Patie and me. That makes her special.

Scene Nine

Jenny, **Liza**, **Tottie**. *Night. Candlelight. They have a candle, a looking-glass, an apple. With lots of shushing, they arrange themselves, so that* **Tottie** *has the candle,* **Jenny** *the glass,* **Liza** *the apple.* **Liza** *places herself in front of, and not too near, the glass. A clock begins to strike twelve. This is what they've been waiting for. Immediately, solemnly,* **Liza** *bites into the apple, throws the bitten-out chunk over her left shoulder.* **Tottie** *wants to retrieve the bite of apple* – **Jenny** *restrains her. They take the apple from* **Liza***, hand her a comb. Ceremoniously she combs her hair, staring all the while into the mirror, peering into the space over her shoulder in the mirror. The others are waiting expectantly,* **Tottie** *tries to look in the glass, obscuring* **Liza***'s own view of it, they signal* **Tottie** *to move away. Suddenly* **Liza** *bursts into excited laughter, doubles up, dances around, gives a 'hooch' of delight.*

Tottie *and* **Jenny** *crowding, cutting each other's lines, in a rush:*

Jenny   Did you see him, Liza?

Tottie   Which one, Liza?

Jenny   Was it the Gyptian?

Tottie Was it Kello?

Jenny Black-eyed Kello?

Liza *still dancing about, laughing, nodding 'yes', clutching at* **Jenny**.

Tottie Do me! My turn!

Jenny (*sternly*) No!

Tottie I want to see my man! Give me an apple! (*She looks for the apple piece that* **Liza** *threw over her shoulder.*)

Jenny Sumph! It's past twelve o the clock! You can't tell fortunes now!

She or **Liza** *blows out the candle.*

You can't see anyone now!

Scene Ten

Liza, **Maggie**, **Sara**, **Tottie**, **Jenny** . . . *and later,* **Ellen**. *They are stopping for a piece-break, milk or water, and bannocks of some kind.* **Maggie** *has brought the food along to the field for them.*

Tottie He was shouting – in the turnip shed. Shouting at the neeps. Nobody there, just neeps.

Maggie It's a speech. For the meeting! He'll be practising his speech.

Jenny For the Soiree!

Liza (*the title – an official one – sounds glamorous to her*) The Plooman's Soiree!

Sara Go on, then, Tottie, tell us – what did he say?

Tottie He said – we are not penny pies.

Liza
'Gentlemen! We are not penny pies
We must continue to press for the six-pound rise!'

Tottie Yes, that's what he said.

Sara Six pound!

Maggie Rowat of Currivale gives farm servants a grand wage, and lost time.

Sara Lost time?

Liza What's that?

Maggie I dinna rightly ken. But he gives them it.

Sara Dunlop of Smiddyhill's promised to mend up his houses. Planks on the floor. *And* in the loft.

Maggie Every year the maisters promise to mend up the houses! But syne it's time for the Speaking, and syne the Hiring, and syne the Flitting – and where are the promises?

Maggie *and* **Sara** Snowed off the dyke!

Sara If we didn't flit every year, they'd have to mend up the houses.

Maggie If the houses were mended up, we wouldn't want to flit ae year.

Sara (*quite cheerful*) Tinklers, that's all we are!

Tottie Penny pies. We are not penny pies.

Maggie A six-pound rise would do me fine, and a new house even finer – but what we really need is an end to the bondage.

Surprise from the others.

(*Slightly abashed.*) Lots of folk are beginning to speak out against the bondage.

Others not convinced.

I've barely a shilling a week to spare for her.

Liza I earn my keep!

Jenny A shilling! Is that all we're worth?

Maggie Barely a shilling for all that food –

Liza – I'm aye starving –

Jenny   Even a horse can't work without food!

Maggie   She takes the bed from my bairns, and the warmth from my fire –

Liza (*furious*)   Where d'you expect me to –

Sara (*restrains her*)   She doesn't mean you – (*To* **Maggie**.) Maggie! – (*To* **Liza**.) It's the bondage she's angry at!

Maggie   Flighty, giddy bits o lassies! Pay no heed to the hind, or his wife!

Liza   I'm not *your* servant!

Maggie   I'm not *your* washerwoman!

Sara   This'll never do now, fraying like – tinklers!

Tottie   Penny pies!

Maggie   Remember Rob Maxwell two year ago at the Hiring? Pleading with a bondager – a woman he didnae ken from Eve – begging her to take the arle as if his very life depended on it!

Sara   Well, but it did. For his ain wife had bairns, and without a female worker who would have hired him? No maister round here.

Maggie   And remember how that young bondager turned out? Remember a' that?

Liza   What?

Maggie   Never you mind. But a poor unsuspecting hind shouldn't have to hire by looks. A sweet face won't shift the sharn.

Liza   And what about us? It works both ways.

Jenny   Ay, both ways. How can we choose a decent hind by his looks?

Maggie   That's just it – the farmer should hire you lassies, not the hind.

Liza   We'd still get picked by our looks.

Maggie Andra's picked by his looks too, come to that.

Liza They'd still pinch our arms and gawp at our legs!

Jenny We'd still have to sleep with the bairns – or worse!

Maggie The maister should hire all the bondagers himself – ay, and lodge them too.

Sara Now, where could he lodge them, Maggie?

Liza In the Big Hoose!

Jenny In the big bed! Oooh-ooh!

Liza We should have a meeting!

Sara Who?

Liza Us! The lassies! There's as many of us as them! More lassies than men, come harvest!

Maggie and **Sara** *shrug off her anger, won't see the point.*

We should make the speeches!

Maggie What do you want? A six-pound rise? And what would you spend it on? Ribbons, ruching? (*To* **Sara**.) Do you know how much this besom owes the draper?

Liza We don't get much!

Maggie I wish I had it. I hunger my bairns, whiles, to feed you! And you spend your money at the draper's!

Jenny We don't get much compared to the men.

Maggie A man's got a family.

Liza Sara's got a family.

Sara Oh, but we're not doing men's work. We canna work like men.

Ellen 'Don't be ridiculous, Ellen,' says the maister. 'We can't do away with the bondage. I can't employ a man who hasn't a woman to work with him. One pair of horse to every fifty acre, one hind for every pair of horse, one bondager for every hind. That's the way it's done,' he says. 'I'm all for progress,' he says, 'but I won't do away with the bondage,' he says. 'We need the women. Who else would do the work? . . . Women's work, for women's pay.'

Liza (*or all, taking phrase by phrase, in turn. She is kirtling up her skirts, putting on the sacking apron*)   Redd up the stables, muck out the byre, plant the tatties, howk the tatties, clamp the tatties. Single the neeps, shaw the neeps, mangle the neeps, cart the neeps. Shear, stook, striddle, stack. Women's work.

Ellen   Muck. A heap of it – higher than your head. Wider than a house. Every bit of it to be turned over. Aired. Rotted. Women's work.

Liza (*forking the dung*)
Shift the sharn, fulzie, muck
Sharn, sharn, fulzie, muck
Shift the sharn, fulzie, muck . . . *etc.*

Ellen (*on top of* **Liza***'s words*)   Muck is gold, says the maister.

Liza (*forking, digging*)
Sharn, sharn, fulzie, muck
Sharn, sharn, fulzie, muck

Ellen   Muck's like kindness, says the maister, it can be overdone.

Liza (*to* **Ellen**)   You mind what it was like, cleaning your claes after this? My new bonnet – it stinks. My claes, my skin.

Sara   It's Maggie who washes your claes.

Liza (*to* **Ellen**)   What was the job you hated most?

Ellen   Howking tatties. I'm long – here – in the back. At the end of the day I used to scraffle on all fours. I couldn't get to my feet till I was halfway down the loan. Can you shear?

Liza   Aye.

Ellen   Striddle?

Liza   Aye!

Ellen   Are you good?

Liza   Aye. It's the corn I love best. It's the whisper it gives when it's ripe for the sickle.

Ellen   I love the speed of it all, the fury. Faster, faster, keep up with the bandster; faster, faster, and better your neighbour. I felt like yon Amazon in the Bible. No one could stop me, if Mabon himself had stood before me, I'd have cut him in two with a swipe o my sickle. I gloried in the shearing. I'll miss the hairst.

Liza and **Ellen** *smile at each other.*

Sara   I remember my mother and her neighbour each had a rig of corn on the village allotment. My mother was gey thrang, all her life. Too much to do, no time to do it. One night, when the corn was ripe, she couldn't sleep. The moon was full. So she went out to shear her corn. And as she sheared, every now and then, she'd take just a bitty from her neighbour's rig, just as much as would make bands to tie her sheaves. Syne she went home and slept the last hour or two till day, glad the work was done. But in the morning, passing the field, she saw she'd reaped the wrong rig, her neighbour's rig. The corn she'd stolen to bind her sheaves was her own corn – and she still had her own rig to shear. O, but she grat! It was a punishment, she said.

Scene Eleven

Maggie, **Liza**, **Sara**. *Evening.* **Sara** *is working quietly – in her garden or her house (sewing? hoeing?), near enough to hear/overhear* **Liza** *and* **Maggie**. **Maggie** *is busy (so is her tongue, she scarcely draws breath during the first part of this scene). She could be churning butter – it calls for steady rhythmic movement, she wouldn't be able to leave her work till the milk was turned.* **Liza** *is not so busy: adding ribbon to her petticoats, or ruching to her bonnet.*

Maggie   You must draw *all* the milk off each milking. Well, I've told you before, it's no use milking if you don't milk her right – she'll draw all the milk that's left back into herself, and come next milking she'll give a bit less –

Liza   Coo, coo, I'm sick o the coo.

Maggie – you'll only get the same next time, as you took from her the time before. We need all the milk she can give. I can't bake flourocks without good cream –

Liza I could eat a coo, I'm starving!

Maggie – Andra's fond of flourocks. *You* eat them fast enough – And what about the teats, Liza? I said wash the teats with alum and water –

Liza Horses – aye. Coos – no.

Maggie – I said to wash the warts on her teats. Poor coo. A' you bondagers are the same. You know nothing of coos, or kitchens or bairns –

Liza Bairns – never!

Maggie The milking's important, Liza, can't you see. I can't feed the family without it!

Liza You've plenty of your own if your coo runs dry.

Maggie (*stops short, at last, for a moment anyway*) Aye, I have. And don't think I'm not proud of it. Oh, you wait. Wait till you're wed. Wait till you've a man to feed –

Liza Oh, wait. You wait. You'll ken! You'll see!

Maggie – Wait till you've bairns. You'll ken. You'll see! Canna bake, canna milk, canna sew, canna spin. Wait till you're wed!

Liza I'm not getting wed. I'll be a cottar wife like Sara.

Sara (*more to herself than to them*) You want to be like Sara? It's day and way for Sara. Every year gets harder for Sara.

Liza (*coming in over Sara's words*) I'm not getting wed. Not yet. Not for years. The sooner you wed, the more bairns you get.

Maggie That's what you wed for – bairns!

Liza Why?

Maggie Why? Why! (*Can't think what to say, can't see why she can't think what to say.*) Why, they keep the roof over you when they're older, that's why. They keep things going. Wull and Tam will soon be half-yins, getting halfpay, and when they're grown there'll be Jim and Drew, and the girls will make bondagers in time. Meg can work with her daddy. Netta can work with Wull or Tam. It'll be grand. We'll can take our pick at the Hiring. Ay, we'll be easy then. Soon enough.

Liza All in the one house – all in the one room? And what about him (*Indicating the cradle.*), he'll not be grown, and Rosie's still wee – and how many more? Easy! You'd be easier without.

Maggie Without what?

Liza Bairns.

Maggie Fields aye need folk.

Liza Bairns for the maister?

Maggie What's a hoose without bairns?

Liza If you think they're so bonny, what are you greeting for?

Maggie Me?

Liza What do you greet for nights?

Maggie No, not me – it must have been one of the wee ones – Rosie cries –

Liza 'Bake, cook, sew, spin, get wed, have bairns.' Natter, natter. Nothing about fighting him off in the night!

Maggie (*a gesture: meaning 'you're havering'*) Now … where was I … what was I going to do next …

Liza I hear you! I hear you nights! Do you think I don't hear you?

Maggie Now, what was I doing …

Liza You sit on by the fire, hoping he'll sleep. You fetch moss from the peat moor to stuff up your legs. I've seen.

Sara (*calling out from her own house, or garden*)   Liza, fetch me some water, would you?

Liza   It's bad enough listening when folk are – happy. But when they're pleading, crying – giving in –

Sara   Liza! Go to the pump for me, there's my lass!

Maggie (*very upset, loathe to admit it to herself*)   What's day is day . . . and night is night.

Sara   Liza!

Liza, *insouciant, unrepentant, fetches some receptacle for water, and goes off to the pump.*

Maggie   . . . and the bairns are my days! (*She starts – or resumes – some piece of work, then stops, goes to the cradle.*) Aye . . . wee lamb . . . my wee burdie . . . (*Picks him up.*) She doesna ken ought. Just a muckle great tawpie, that's all she is. (*Begins to nurse the baby.*) Dinna go to sleep my burdie. Tak your fill.

It is she who is being comforted by the nursing, rather than the baby.

Now . . . Now . . . I ken where I am now. I canna feel dowie when you tug like that. A' the bairns at the breast. A' the folk in the fields. A' the bonny folk. A good harvest is a blessing to all. Aye. That's right. Tak yer fill, burdie, I ken who I am when you're there.

Scene Twelve

Liza, **Tottie**, *all.* **Liza** *is waltzing – humming, or lala-ing the tune ('Logie o Buchan'). Then starts to make up words for the tune, dancing hesitantly, searching hesitantly for words. Sings some or all of this.*

Liza
O, the plooman's so bonny wi black curly hair
He dances so trig and his smile is just rare
His arms are so strong as he birls me awa
His black eyes are bonny and laughing and bra

34 **Bondagers**

His name it is Kello, the best o them a'
His name it is Kello, the best o them a'

Waltzing with an imaginary partner now, more confident, repeating the song more confidently . . .

A laugh heard from **Tottie,** *who has been hiding, watching. She appears, kissing her own arm with grotesque kissing noises, sighing, petting noises.* **Liza,** *annoyed, gives her a shove or tries to –* **Tottie** *shoves back, hard.*

Tottie   Tinkler, tailor, beggar – *Kello!* (*More kissing noises.*) Tinkler, tailor, beggar – *lover!*

Liza   Tak yer hook, you – go on.

Tottie   I looked in the glass. I looked in the glass too. It was twelve o clock, so I saw. I saw my man. You know who I saw?

Liza   You haven't a glass. Jenny's the only one with a glass. Away wag yer mou somewhere else. Go on!

Tottie   Jenny went with the saddler. I saw them in the rigs. Not our rigs. The lang syne rigs up by the moor. You can hide up there, the furrows are deep. The ghosts'll get them if they don't watch out. Her claes were way up. Woosh! She's getting wed to the saddler. That's what you do! Woosh! (. . .) I've seen you too. You went with the Gyptian. In the turnip house.

Liza   I never did. I was dancing, that's all. He was showing me the steps. And he's not a Gyptian.

Tottie   Woosh!

Liza   Daftie! Come on, I'll show you the steps. Come on, come here.

Tottie   I know the steps!

Liza   I want to go over the steps. If you don't know them right, no one will ask you. You want to dance at the kirn, don't you?

Liza holds out her arms, but **Tottie** *declines to dance with her.* **Liza** *starts waltzing again, singing.* **Tottie** *watches for a while, then* *suddenly breaks into a raucous clog (or boot) dance, in fast reel or jig time: rough, spirited, noisy. And, like* **Liza**, *sings her own accompaniment*:

Tottie
Liza loves the plooman
Bonnie black-eyed plooman
Kello is the plooman
O, he's no a tinkler
O, he's no a mugger
O, he's no a Gyptian
He's a black-eyed plooman
Bonnie black-eyed plooman, *etc.*

Which kills **Liza**'s *waltz. She stares amazed –* **Tottie**'s *dancing may lack finesse, but it's wholehearted, makes you want to dance with her.*

The others appear, join in. Someone bangs the ground with a graip (or hoe) handle, beating time, they are all singing **Tottie**'s *rhythm now, same tune, same lines, but each singing different lines to each line of the music. The dance is becoming the kirn, has led into the kirn. It stops abruptly*:

Voices *(toasts, asides, conversation)*
The kirn, the kirn, the kirn, the kirn
What a folk/a'body's here/mind the bairns
A good harvest/best for years/best in my time

Tottie *(listing the repertoire of dances)*   Reel o Tulloch, ribbon dance, pin reel, polka

Voices
All the corn standing and none to lift
I can't stay late because of the bairns
Will you look at Marjie's petticoats!
The saddler's shed his hair doon the middle!

Tottie   Tullogorum, petronella, strathespey, scotch reel

Voices
A good harvest's the envy of none
And a blessing to all

(*Toast.*) Welcome to the maister
(*Toast.*) Thanks to the maister for the harvest home
And the use of the barn
And the beer and the baps
We've a good maister
(*Toast.*) To the maister
And a better mistress
(*Toast.*) To the mistress
Health and Prosperity
A good harvest is a blessing to all
And the envy of none

They shush each other to silence as someone starts to sing (maybe Burns, the song entitled 'Somebody':)

My heart is sair – I darena tell –
My heart is sair for somebody;
I could wake a winter night
For the sake o somebody.
Ohon! for somebody!
O-hey! for somebody!
I could range the world around,
For the sake o somebody!

Ye Powers that smile on virtuous love,
O, sweetly smile on somebody!
Frae ilka danger keep him free,
And send me safe my somebody.
Ohon! for somebody!
O-hey! for somebody!
I wad do – what wad I not?
For the sake o somebody!

Scene Thirteen

Jenny, Liza, Maggie, Tottie, Sara. *Dawn, or just after, the morning after the kirn.* **Jenny** *and* **Liza** *arriving home, fits of giggles. High from lack of sleep and the night's events.* **Maggie** *has heard them coming, she's already up – splashing her face with water? fetching water? something – and 'nursing her wrath'.*

Maggie I'll thraw your neck when I come to you, lass. I'll dadd your lugs. I'll skelp you blue.

Liza We were only dancing!

Maggie Dancing! He was dragging you down the loan!

Jenny He'd had a drop! They'd all had a drop.

Maggie Gyptians! Steal the clothes off your back – and a whole lot more!

Liza Kello's not a Gyptian.

Jenny It was the kirn, Maggie.

Liza We were dancing!

Maggie Where to? Coldstream?

Renewed giggles.

And for the love of the Lord, stop that laughing. You cackled and screeched all through the kirn!

Jenny She wasn't going to Coldstream *really*! She wasn't getting wed or anything!

Liza (*mockingly*) Oooh-ooh! Buckled up at Coldstream!

Maggie You weren't? Were you? By, you'd see – !

Liza You'd lose your bondager if I got wed. That's all that bothers you.

Maggie Get ready for work, go on, the pair of you. The steward won't brook lateness after the kirn. Especially not after the kirn. He'll have a thumping head on him this morning. And not the only one. Gin you were mine – I'd shake you, lass!

Sara has appeared, been milking her cow or fetching water or firewood.

Sara Is Tottie not up yet?

They stare at her blankly.

Sara Still sleeping with the bairns, is she?

Maggie *shakes her head, is about to say 'no'.*

Sara   I left her last night dancing with the bairns.

Maggie   Well, she wsn't with me, Sara.

Sara (*worried, but not unduly*)   I thought she was sleeping at your place. Now where can she be?

Maggie   The hayloft, probably.

Jenny and Liza exchange looks.

Sara   She didn't want to leave with me. She wanted to dance.

Jenny   She followed us a way.

Sara   You've seen her then – ?

Jenny   Last night.

Sara   Well, but now, where is she now?

Maggie (*angry, to Liza and/or Jenny*)   You should have kept an eye on her.

Jenny	Why?
Liza	She's a pest.
Jenny	Traipsing after us.

Maggie   She's been girny lately. Thrawn.

Sara   She's been having bad days.

Liza   What's the fuss? She never goes far. She's too daft to get far.

They catch sight of Tottie.

Sara   Tottie, burdie, where have you been? Come here. You're a bad girl, going off like that, where have you been?

Tottie (*triumphant, but wary too – keeps her distance*)   I've been married.

'Ooh-ing' or giggles again from Liza and Jenny.

Sara   Oh, it's a notion she takes. Like the dancing.

Maggie (*to Jenny, Liza*)   She was with you, then?

Sara   Where have you been, Tottie?

Tottie I've been with my man. Getting wed. Liza wouldn't go. He didn't want her anyway.

Each time they approach her she withdraws.

Jenny You've never been to Coldstream and back, not without wings.

Liza You can't wed, you're not sixteen.

Tottie I'm not the bairnie now! I know things. I'm wed.

Maggie It's their fault, putting ideas in her head.

Liza } Us!
Jenny } She wasn't with us!

Tottie I was! I was. They were going to Coldstream brig, they were laughing and dancing, they were having a wedding. I wanted to go too. But they shouted at me, Liza and Jenny and Kello and Dave, and Dave threw a stone. So I hid. Then I heard them running across the field, Liza and Jenny, running and stopping to have a bit laugh, and running and stopping and laughing and running. But the ploomen didn't run cos they'd had too much ale, they couldn't loup the dyke, they stayed in the loan. So I went and asked them could I go to Coldstream instead, and Kello said yes.

Liza Kello.

Jenny You've never been to Coldstream!

Liza She's making it up, she talks like that all the time.

Tottie I'm going to have a clock and a dresser and a bed. And a baby.

The silence gratifies her.

Liza Who said?

Tottie *starts laughing, almost dancing (or lolling about in the hay, as* **Ellen** *did earlier), hugging herself with satisfaction – at last night's, as well as this morning's, attention.*

Maggie What did he do? Tottie? Which one was it, and what did he do?

Sara   There's blood on her skirt.

Maggie (*slapping at, or shoving at* **Jenny** *or* **Liza**, *whichever is nearest*)   Your fault, bitches!

As she speaks the farmyard bell – maybe just two iron bars banged together – is heard in the distance.

Maggie   That's the steward in the yard. You're late. Go on, the pair of you, hurry up, go on. No sense everyone being late.

Sara   Tell the steward we're both sick, Tottie and me. Tell him we're sick.

Maggie   And Jenny – both of you – keep your gob shut!

Liza (*to* **Tottie**)   Was it Kello?

Maggie   Tak your hook, Liza!

Tottie (*calling after her in triumph*)   You're the bairnie now, Liza!

Liza *and* **Jenny** *go slowly towards the field, collect their hoes, tie on their headhankies, aprons, etc.*

Tottie   It was Kello I saw in the glass. Yon night I took a loan of Jenny's glass.

Maggie *and* **Sara** *say nothing, don't know what to say – to* **Tottie**, *to each other.*

Tottie   He said we hadn't got all night, we'd never get to Coldstream, we should go in the rigs. We were wed in the rigs. Lift your claes! Woosh! I wanted a look at his prick, but I couldn't see right, it was still half dark. And he never lay me doon at all, he pushed me agin the stack. 'We'll smoor the fleas together,' he says. 'It canna hurt if we smoor a wheen fleas.' But it hurt. I'm hurt.

But just when she seems distressed and ready to be comforted, she starts laughing again, excited, gleeful.

Liza   They'll tell the steward and the maister.

Jenny (*to* **Liza**)   What'll they do to that Kello, eh? What'll they *not* do!

Maggie   There's always trouble after the kirn!

Jenny (*looking to the fields*)   They're ploughing already. I can see the horses. *He's* turning up the stubble, your Kello –

Liza   Not mine!

Maggie   Go to work, Sara. I'll see to her now. Leave her here with me. If you don't work, you don't get paid. And the steward'll be angry if you're not in the field, it'll make him angrier at Tottie.

Sara (*more angry than sad, for once*)   At *Tottie*?

But **Sara** *can't go*.

Jenny (*to* **Liza**)   What'll you say when you see him, Kello?

Liza   I won't see him – I won't look!

Jenny   If he speaks to –

Liza   I'll spit!

Maggie (*looking to fields*)   They're ploughing already. Ploughing for winter.

Sara   Come home now, bairnie!

Tottie   Not the bairnie now!

Maggie   Trouble – it comes like the first nip of frost. Sure as frost after harvest.

Liza   I wish it was last night again. I wish it was the kirn still.

Maggie   Sure as winter.

Jenny   I wish the summer would last for ever.

Liza   I wish we were still dancing!

Act Two

Scene One

It is dark, at first we barely see the characters on stage. The different sections of chorus here come fast on top of each other, sections actually overlapping – until **Maggie** *and* **Sara** *speak individually, in character.*

A single voice (*tune: traditional*)
Up in the morning's no for me
Up in the morning early
When a' the hills are covered in snow
Then it is winter fairly ... (*Last line more spoken than sung.*)

Voices (*in a spoken round*)
When a' the hills are covered in snow
Then it is winter fairly ...

As the round finishes, voices still saying 'Winter ... winter ... winter ... '

A burst of noise: a rattle of tin cans, or sticks clattering together, or a stick drumming on tin – or something like. (It was Hogmanay, not Hallowe'en, when kids went guising in the Borders.)

A child (*calling out in a mock scary way*)   OOooooh!

A child (*calling out, merry*)
We're only some bits o bairns come oot to play
Get up – and gie's oor Hogmanay!

Some laughter, children's laughter. The rattle/drumming noise. If possible an impression of the laughter fading to distance – as if the children have retreated, and the adults, and adult worries, are coming to the centre of the stage.

Voices (*singly, in turn*)
Cold wind: snow wind
Small thaw: mair snaw
The snow wreaths

The feeding storm
The hungry flood

Sara's and **Maggie**'s *speeches here more definite, more individual.*

Sara   The dread of winter. All summer long, the dread of it.
Like a nail in the door that keeps catching your hand. Like a
nip in the air in the midst of the harvest.

A voice (*whispery, echoey*)   Cold wind: snow wind.

Maggie (*brisk, busy*)   There's beasts to be fed, snaw or blaw!

Voice   Cold. Ice. Iron.

Maggie (*with a certain satisfaction*)   A green yule makes a fat
kirkyard!

As **Tottie** *starts speaking, light comes on her. Her voice gets louder.
She is brandishing a graip – maybe there are tin cans or something else
tied to it that make a noise when she brandishes. She is swathed for
winter (as are the rest of the cast here, but not quite so wildly) – straw-
rope leggings, her arms covered in extra knitted oversleeves; fingerless
mitts, shawl, the headhankie pulled protectively well around the face. A
right tumshie-bogle.*

Tottie (*voice becomes less childish, harsher, more violent as she
recites*)
Get up auld wife and shake your feathers
Ye needna think that we're a' wheen beggars
We're only some bits o bairns come oot to play
Get up – and gie's oor Hogmanay!

*Aggressive now, hitting out maybe – whanging the straw bales/stack/
hedgerow with the graip or just beating about with it, or beating the
ground.*

Hogmanay – Hogmanick
Hang the baker ower the stick
When the stick begins to break
Take another and break his back

Tottie, Liza, Sara – and **Maggie**, *who talks with them, but has
work to do in her own 'home area'.*

Sara   Tottie!

Tottie No!

Sara We'll be late for the field, Tottie.

Tottie I want to play.

Maggie Don't be daft, now.

Tottie (*with menace*) Not!

Maggie The maister'll be after you.

Tottie A' the men are after Tottie!

Sara Tie up yer claes, we're going to the field.

Tottie I'm playing!

Sara We've to work, Tottie. No work, no shillings.

Maggie You're too big to play!

Tottie I'm married now!

Maggie Leave her be. What's the use when she's this way?

Sara If I leave her be she'll go deaving the men.

Tottie I'm going guising. Going to guise the ploomen in the chamber.

Sara No, you're not. You're not to go there, Tottie. Leave the men alone.

Tottie (*violent. She's still apart from them, by herself*)
'Hogmanay, Hogmanick
Take another and break his back' . . .
A'body wants Tottie. A' the men are after Tottie.

Liza *watching all this, watching* **Sara** *and* **Tottie**, *miserable for herself and them.*

Maggie Best leave her for now. Best get moving. You'll make the steward angry if you're late – aye, and the maister. No work, no pay.

Sara *goes towards the field.* **Tottie** *sulking.*

Maggie (*with venom, she's meaning* **Liza**) Dirt! . . . Dirt!

Liza, *utterly miserable, follows* **Sara** *towards the field.*

Scene Two

Tottie *by the stacks/bales.*

Tottie (*a slow, sour version of her former jig/song*)
Tottie loves the plooman
Tottie's black-eyed plooman
Kello is the plooman

Throws herself against the stack, beats at it a bit with her body, her arms, her fists . . .

Not fair. Wasn't there. Not fair. Didn't come . . .
'Away up the moor, Tottie,' he says. 'I'll meet you up on the moor.'
But he didnae. Kello.
There was a man there, but it wasnae him.
Twixt me and the sun. Just the one man.
He was stood in the rigs, the lang syne rigs.
'A week's work done in a day,' he cries.
'We don't need you now!
We don't need folk. We don't need horses.
Machines without horses.
We've plenty bread now,' he cries.
'Too much bread.'
He was pleased. He was laughing.
But I wasnae feared. (*She's laughing a bit, it pleases her.*)
For he wasnae the ghost.
I was! I was the ghost!

Voices (*whilst speaking these lines, they are moving into position, still muffled in headhankies, mitts, etc., still 'hauden-doon' by winter. Spoken quite matter-of-factly, either singly, turn by turn, or in unison*)
Barley means bread
Pease means bread
Oats means bread
Wheat means bread
Corn means bread

Tottie (*in the middle of the above, on top of their words – the voices do not pause*)
'We've plenty bread now,' he cries.
'Too much bread.'

Voices
Never enough bread
Give us this day our daily bread
The bread of carefulness

Tottie 'Too much bread now! Mountains!' he cries.

Voice(s)   The bread of progress!

Scene Three

Ellen (*polite teatime voice – a teapot or cakestand? – she's talking to the foreigners visiting the show farm of Blacksheils*)   Progress? Progress! The key to progress is rotation: Maister Elliott's six-course rotation. Famed throughout the land; throughout Europe. Corn, potatoes, turnips, and swedes, clover, and rye grass, with a good stock of sheep and cattle. Sixty tons of farm manure. Twelve hundredweight of artificials. Wheat yields – up! Potato yields – up! The rent? – up! – naturally. Raised by the Marquis according to our yields. Rotation! Rotation of course applies also to the workforce. On farms of this size we have to be exact. Twenty men and eight women in winter, eighteen extra women and boys in summer. The steward can't do with less, the master can't pay for more.

(*Not talking to the visitors here.*) If Jimmy Eagan's too frail now to work,
Then he and his family must move elsewhere,
For his house is needed for a younger hind,
And his wife and three daughters are surplus to requirements.
If Tam Neil's lad is ready for the fields,
The family will have to seek a new place at the Hiring,
We've too many young boys at Blacksheils already,
We don't need more half-yins,

We need more hinds,
We need more bondagers and unmarried ploughmen.

(*To the visitors again.*) Of course, they never move far . . . ten, fifteen miles . . . They're used to it. Some welcome it . . . 'So long as it's dry for the flitting!'

(*No longer addressing the visitors.*) 'Please God: Keep them dry for the flitting.' . . . He's a fair man, the maister. He'd have built a new row of houses by now – if it wasn't for the Marquis raising the rent. 'I overlook small faults in a good workman,' says the maister. 'I've lived here all my life,' he says. 'I know this place like I know my own hand. I know the Border peasant: honest, industrious, godfearing . . .'

He never knew me, never knew my name even, till I set my cap at him. The first year of marriage, I still had the face of a bondager: white below, where the kerchief had been tied, the top of my cheeks and my nose dirt brown. The ladies stared, and smiled behind their fans. But I'm all pale now, I'm a proper lady now.

Not once has he asked me what it was like: to live in the row, to work in the fields. Not once . . . They've made a lady of me now.

Scene Four

Maggie, Tottie, Sara, Liza . . . *and* **Ellen** *later. All working, or about to.* **Maggie** *working in, or for, her own house.* **Liza** *filling buckets or a barrow with neeps to feed the beasts (or crushing the neeps in the crusher).* **Sara** *helping* **Tottie** *to 'breech her claes', i.e. kirtle up her skirts, so that they're almost like trousers, ready for work.*

Sara   Has he spoken to Andra, the maister?

Maggie   No. Not yet. Has he spoken to you?

Sara (*shakes her head*)   No. Not yet. Not to anyone yet. Not that I've heard. (*Without conviction.*) Well, there's time . . .

Liza   There's hardly any time. It's past Hogmanay.

A pause. Uneasy.

Sara   Maister Elliott always speaks well before the Hiring. He's good that way.

Maggie   Not long till the Hiring now.

Liza   First Monday in February.

Uneasy pause.

Maggie   He's bound to keep some on. The steward; the herd. And he's well pleased with Andra, he'll be speaking to Andra. (*To* **Sara**.) Ellen'll see that you're kept on, don't fret.

Sara   Tottie's had bad days. Too many bad days.

Maggie   And who's to blame? Kello. Well, they won't keep him on, that's for sure. It's a wonder he wasn't sent packing before – straight after the kirn! Mind, the same could be said for some other – dirt!

Sara   That's not right, Maggie, that's not fair!

Maggie   You don't know the half of it. Don't know the half of her! Flaunty piece of – dirtery!

Sara *wants to smooth this, but can't.*

Maggie, **Sara**, **Liza**, *all speaking and shouting at once here:*

Maggie (*to* **Liza**)   Her father must be turning in his grave. Dirt. If the maister only knew, he'd send her packing. Dirt – that's all she is.

Liza (*incoherent, upset*)   My father – aye, he must – at you – at you and your man. What do you expect me to do – what? If my father knew – if Steenie was here – he'd – if he – it's not right – it's not.

Maggie   Just like her mother. Maisie Kerr – no better than she should be. Tinkler trash!

Sara   That's not true, Maggie, that's not true at all!

Liza   Liar! That's a lie!

Ellen   What's all this? All this noise? Haven't you work enough to keep busy? The maister's sick of all this clamjamfray. Where's Tottie – Tottie? – Tottie, come here –

Tottie *comes, without enthusiasm.* **Ellen** *hugs her, but she doesn't reciprocate.*

Ellen   Why haven't you been working? Bad girl. Wild girl! (*Says this nicely, cajolingly, but* **Tottie,** *sulky, is trying to break away.*) You used to be a good worker, Tottie. You've got to be good. Hey, now, promise me, now – you'll be a good girl now.

Tottie *retreats to stack, bale, somewhere.*

(*To* **Sara.**) The steward's been grumbling to the maister. She deaves all the men, she throws herself at Kello.

Maggie   Kello shouldn't be here. They should have sent him away.

Ellen   Yes. I know.

Maggie   Then why did they not?

Ellen   Because she wouldn't say. Tottie wouldn't say. (*To* **Tottie.**) You should have told them, Tottie, you should have told them what happened to you.

Maggie   She said it all to us. Don't they believe it? There was blood on her claes.

Ellen   I know.

Maggie   He should have been punished.

Ellen (*knowing how feeble this is*)   They did punish him, the men.

Maggie   Oh – they douked him in the trough, and kicked him round the yard. But they feel sorry for him now. Some of the lads admire him, almost, some of the lassies even. It's Tottie they're angry at now.

Liza *very silent, very subdued – and very resentful.*

Sara   He changed Tottie. He stole her.

Maggie   They laugh and swear at her now.

Ellen 'I keep a steward to manage my workers.' That's all the maister says, that's all he'll say. 'I won't keep a dog and bark for myself.'

Maggie He barks when it's lassies causing the trouble. He sent Minnie packing . . . almost before we'd time to find out why!

Ellen And the steward won't budge. 'It takes two,' he says. 'Takes two to smoor the fleas.' You know how they are – maisters, stewards – they leave things be, till the turn of the year. They leave it till the Speaking, and let the bad ones go. Leave it till the Hiring, and let them go.

Maggie (*with some satisfaction*) No one'll hire Kello. That's for sure!

Ellen I wouldn't be so certain. He's good with the horses, he's a hero with horses.

Maggie (*with a venomous look at* **Liza**) Folk like that are left till last at the Hiring! Lads or lassies!

Sara It's us who'll get left, Tottie and me.

Ellen You won't need to go the Hiring, Sara. You can stay on here, you know that surely. But see she behaves. If she won't do any work, at least keep her quiet – and away from the men. For the maister won't stand for all this – nonsense.

Sara *obviously feels this is easier said than done.*

Ellen She throws up her skirts, she rushes at Kello, the other men have to pull her away.

Sara (*very quietly*) He changed Tottie, he stole her.

Maggie If she hated him now – if she feared him, even – well, that would make sense.

Sara She's angry at him – but not that way.

Ellen You know what they say? 'Well, no wonder,' they say. 'No wonder what happened, just look at the way she behaves, poor Kello, poor man, it wasn't his fault, he'd had a few, mind, why not, at the kirn, and what was she doing there out in the field – asking for it.' That's what they say.

Sara   I know.

Maggie (*going off, brisk, busy*)   Not the only one asking for it. And not just in the fields, either! Sleekit piece of dirtery!

Sara (*to* **Tottie***; as she talks, she fetches* **Tottie***, and ushers her reluctantly off*)   We'll spoil a few moudies in the far field, Tottie, eh? You like doing that. Fetch your hoe, we'll give the moudieworps a gliff!

Ellen (*she has been aware of* **Liza***'s reactions, and the vibes from* **Maggie** *throughout this scene*)   Liza!

Liza   I've the beasts to feed.

Ellen (*signals* **Liza** *to come nearer*)   There's Mary and Jenny to see to the beasts. Tell them I needed you up at the House. It's no more than the truth – there's flax to be spun!

Liza (*miserable, awkward, won't meet* **Ellen***'s eye*)   Can't spin. I don't want to spin.

Ellen (*though never sentimental, touched now by* **Liza***'s misery*)   Don't listen to Maggie, what she said about your mother, it isn't true. She's jealous, that's all. Your father was fierce – but a'body liked your mother.

Liza   How would you know?

Ellen   Steenie told me. Over and over.

Liza *wants very much to go.*

Ellen   Liza. It wasn't your fault. About Kello and Tottie. You're not to blame. Don't let them blame you. Jenny's not blamed. She holds up her head. Don't let them blame you.

Liza (*frustrated, near to tears*)   It's not just that . . . It's *her*!

Ellen   Maggie?

Liza   *Him*!

Ellen   Kello?

Liza *shakes her head.*

Ellen Andra?

Liza *nods.*

Ellen (*incredulous*) Andra!

Liza (*blurting this, chopping it up*) It's not my fault. It's not. Just because I – because – because of Kello – since the kirn – Maggie – they all think – they all think I'm – word gets round – it's not my fault – I haven't done anything . . .

Ellen (*disbelief – not tragically shocked, because she can't take Andra all that seriously – maybe a hint of mirth already in her voice*) Andra.

Liza (*upset*) She won't – I can't help hearing them at night – and then he – I hate it, hearing them – she won't let him, she won't touch him – and then he – he comes and stands by the other bed. I keep the curtains drawn, I hug the bairns close, the two on the outside, and the wee one between me and the wall – but they sleep like the dead – he stands there, I can hear him – *she* can hear him, that's the worst, she can hear him, I hear her listening – but it's not my fault – it's not my fault – it's not . . .

Ellen But he doesn't – does he? – *Andra?* What does he do?

Liza Nothing. He stands there. Breathing.

Ellen *can no longer hold in her laughter, fairly snorts with mirth.*

Liza (*outraged at this response*) It isn't funny. It isn't my fault.

Ellen Andra! It would be like going to bed with a tumshie! (*Beginning to laugh again.*)

Liza (*in self-defence*) He isn't in my bed. (*Almost in defence of him.*) I don't think he's a tumshie! He's got awful bonny legs.

Ellen Oh?

Liza I've spied them through the curtains.

Ellen Ah.

Liza I like working with Andra. That wall-eyed mare, the one that kicks, she was ramming me tight against the stable wall, I was losing my breath, but Andra came along and roared and whacked her, he showed me how to roar and whack, she's been quiet with me since.

Ellen (*laughter threatening again*)   Ummm.

Liza   I don't want him in my bed, whatever Maggie says. I don't want him at all. I'm not a bad girl.

Ellen   I know that, Liza. I know you're not bad. (*Without remorse, quite fondly.*) Ellen Rippeth was bad, Ellen Rippeth-that-was . . . I was douce with Steenie, though, I wasn't bad to Steenie . . . Have you heard from Steenie?

Liza *shakes her head.*

Ellen   Saskatchewan. Are they douce there, I wonder?

Liza   You sent him away.

Ellen (*brisk*)   Thistles!

Liza   Steenie left because of you.

Ellen   Bonnets! He set off for Canada like you set off for Coldstream brig – he never made up his mind – he'd no mind to make up. You're two of a kind – you and your brother – fresh pats of butter still waiting on the stamp. He was ower young, Steenie. I didn't love him, Liza.

Liza (*muttering*)   You don't love the maister, either.

Ellen   What?

Liza   But you love the maister, do you?

Ellen (*very quietly*)   Almost. Almost.

A pause. Each lost in her own thoughts – of the maister; of Kello.

Liza   Kello can rid the maister's black mare – make it dance, and turn in a ring. He stands on its rump, whilst it circles around, he keeps his balance, he takes off his jacket, his waistcoat, his kerchief. (*She is moving, dancing really, as she recalls watching Kello, in the summer, in the paddock.*) . . . A red-spotted kerchief. He aye keeps his balance, the mare canters round, and around, and around, and when Kello jumps off, he turns in the air, right round in the air, and lands on his feet

. . . A red-spotted kerchief . . . His eyes are aye laughing, he dances so trig. He showed me the steps. He stroked my hair.

Ellen Tinkler, sorner, seducer – thief!

Liza (*taken aback; then braving it out*) I know.

Ellen That's all right then, so long as you know. The maister locks the doors at night to keep him away from the dairymaids. So now he meets with the hedger's wife instead – when he's not walking over to Langriggs at night. The parlourmaid there – they meet in the woods. Bella Menteith. Huh! Who would have thought! Well, she's no chicken – and so perjink!

It's a kick in the teeth for **Liza**. **Ellen** *didn't mean to say so much.*

Liza (*face-saving; lying*) I knew all that! A'body kens that!

Liza *goes.*

Scene Five

Ellen, Maggie, Tottie. **Tottie** *appears – maybe been hiding nearby for a while.*

Ellen (*softly; taking account of* **Tottie**'s *presence, but not directly to her*) A'body kens that. Don't they, Tottie?

Tottie (*ditto: not directly to* **Ellen** *at this point*) 'I'll meet you,' he says. He keeps on saying – 'Away up the moor – down by the mill – along by Craig Water – I'll meet you there, soon – I'll meet you there later.' But he doesnae.

Ellen You don't want to see Kello, Tottie. He's a bad man.

Tottie Yes, he is.

Ellen Then you must leave him alone.

Tottie *still has her hoe, she's been hoeing down molehills. She attacks the ground, or something, haybale, something, with her hoe.*

Tottie Foxton field's plagued with moudies – moudie hillocks all over the field. Ten, two, a hundred moudies! Hogmanany, Hogmanick

Find the moudie and break its neck
Find its hillock and ding it doon
Ding! Dang! – BANG! – Seven hillocks, seven moudies!
(*Well aware of* **Ellen**, *half an eye on* **Ellen**.)
Moudiewort, moudiewort, run to the Tweed
For your hillock's danged doon, and we all want you dead
Ding, dang – damn! (*Repeats this with quieter pleasurable
concentration.*) Damnation! Damn! Damn!

But **Ellen** *is walking away* (*maybe not right offstage*).

Hell! Damn! A hundred moudies! Yes, he's bad. I know
where he bides. He bides in the chamber up above the new
stables. He's to fetch me a clock, still. And a bed. (*She's by the
cradle now.*) Hasn't he, babby? Eh? Wee babby. Bee-baw-
babbity.

Maggie *bustling in:*

Maggie   Now then, Tottie, keep away from wee Joe. You
shouldn't be here – you've work to do. Mind what Mistress
Ellen told you.

Tottie   I'm minding the babby.

Maggie   No, no. Not now. Take that hoe out of here.
You're not to mind the babby any more, he's – he's too big
for you to mind now.

Tottie   He's not. I'm bigger.

Maggie (*losing patience; has the baby in her arms now, waiting for*
Tottie *to go*)   Away you go now, Tottie, get that hoe out of
here!

Tottie *gives the cradle a push, maybe with her hoe, and goes, leaving
the cradle rocking.*

Maggie, *still holding the baby, follows* **Tottie** *a little way, but not
offstage, to make sure she's really going.*

Scene Six

Ellen, Maggie, Sara.

Ellen (*not talking directly to* **Sara** *yet – nor to* **Maggie**)   I like the idea of a winter baby. Swaddled in shawls. I'd feed him in bed by the light of the fire. I'd keep him safe from the feeding storms. When spring burst on us, he'd be fat as a lamb, he'd laugh at the leaves.

Maggie (*muttering*)   Lie in bed? All right for some! (*Busy, busy . . . self-righteousness increasing.*) Lying in bed! With a baby to look after? (*Seems to calm down . . . and then it gets to her again. With scorn and envy.*) Lying in bed! Huh!

She goes.

Meanwhile **Sara** *appears, with some quiet kind of work, maybe knitting (she would be knitting as she walked).*

Ellen (*to* **Sara**)   What do I have to take, Sara? What do I have to do? Don't say: 'Time enough!' Don't say: 'Be patient!' I need a child now! Not for me – well, not for me only – for the maister! (. . .) Sara?

But **Sara** *can't think what to say.*

It was your mother brought me into the world. She knew all the cures. My mother always said she did. You know them, too, don't you?

Sara   Be happy, Nell. You were happy as a lark, once. And so was the maister.

Ellen   He has things on his mind. Yields per acre, tiles for drainage . . . mortgage for mortgage . . . I don't know what. I'm useless in that great house! Dressing up; pouring tea. His mother minds the house, Betty Hope minds me. I'd shift the sharn if it'd help; mangle the neeps, feed the beasts. I watch him at his desk, writing, counting. He doesn't even know I've come into the room. He breaks my heart. I only want it for him. I'm plump, I'm greedy, I'm healthy! Damn it, why can't I swell? It happens soon enough for those who don't want it, who don't even think about it!

Sara   Then don't think about it, Nell.

Exasperation from **Ellen**.

There's time.

More exasperation.

Be patient!

Ellen   Sara!

Sara   And don't let him sit at his desk all night. You can't fall for a baby while he sits at his desk!

They laugh.

Ellen   (. . .) There's a herb. It cures a'thing, my mother used to say. It grows round these parts. I don't know its name. But it looked like a docken, I remember she said that.

Sara *shakes her head very slightly, as she continues knitting or whatever.*

Ellen   You know about it, don't you? You know where it grows?

Sara   It cured cuts and wounds. We put the leaves on the wound, and bandaged them round. I never knew it to fail for things like that. For sickness too, and fevers, and wasting.

Ellen   Barrenness?

Sara *(gently)*   Nell –

Ellen   Tell me where it grows. I'll fetch some. I'll dig it up. Tell me what to do with it. Eat it? Wear it? I'll wrap myself in it from head to heel.

Sara   It used to grow at Craig's Pool. It never had a name. 'The leaves by Craig Water', that's what we cried it. But – I'm not sure it would have cured barrenness, Nell –

Ellen   I could try.

Sara   You aren't barren, Nell – you're spun dizzy with nerves. You just need to –

Ellen   Craig's Pool – on the crook of the river?

Sara   The leaves don't grow there now.

Ellen   Where else do they grow?

Sara   That's the only place we ever knew of. But they don't grow there now. The maister had a wall built, some years ago – to keep the river from flooding the fields. He had the bank raised. They moved tons of earth. And built a braw dyke, and a paving on the bank so we could wash the linen. (. . .) Nobody thought. We used the leaves all the time – your mother was right, we used them for a'thing . . . well . . . (*Partly her sensible opinion, and partly trying to comfort* **Ellen** *in her dismay.*) not so much for babies, Nell, some women tried, but I don't –

Ellen   I could have tried. I could have tried.

Sara   Nobody thought to save any of the roots. Nobody gave it any thought . . .

Scene Seven

All (except **Ellen***).* **Tottie** *brandishing a letter,* **Liza***, desperate, furious, trying to get it back. A silent, quite vicious struggle, shoving, wrestling, pinching, kicking. And* **Tottie** *wins.*

Liza   Give it me.

Tottie   No.

Liza   It's mine.

Tottie   No.

Liza   It's not yours.

Tottie   Sas-katch-e-wan.

Liza   It's not yours.

Tottie   My daddy's been away for a hundred year.

Liza   You can't read anyway.

Tottie   I can so, I can.
Collop Monday,

Pancake Tuesday,
Ash Wednesday,
Bloody Thursday,
Lang Friday,
Hey for Saturday afternoon;
Hey for Sunday at twelve o clock,
Whan a' the plum puddings jump out o the pot.

Throughout this recitation **Liza** *is trying to shut her up, shout her down:*

Liza That's not reading. You can't read. Daftie! You can't read, Tottie!

Tottie *is upset.* **Liza** *beginning – slightly – to take pity on her, but still irritated and fearful for her letter. A moment's pause.* **Tottie** *gets out the letter – keeping it well away from* **Liza**'s *snatching hands, begins to 'read' it:*

Tottie *('reading' the letter)*
'Here's tae ye a' yer days
Plenty meat and plenty claes
Plenty porridge and a horn spoon
And another tattie when a's done.' (. . .) I can so, I can read.

Liza Here. I'll read it to you. (. . .) It's a story. There's a story in the letter – from Steenie, my brother. I'll read you the story.

Very slowly **Tottie** *gives in, gives* **Liza** *the letter. As* **Liza** *opens the letter* **Tottie** *suddenly changes mood, all excitement, all smiles, jumps, dances about, laughing, yelling, yelling at the top of her voice.*

Tottie Hey-ey! Oooo-oh! Hey-ey! Liza's got a letter. Liza's reading a letter. A letter. A story. A story. A letter. Sas-katch-e-wan!

They all come forward, as for a story (it is, for them).

Liza *(reads)* 'Dear Sister: I am writing letting you know I am in good health. The country is good if a man keeps his health. The land costs eleven shillings and thruppence an acre, but we must take up our axes and cut down the trees. Should he not take land, a man gets four shillings a day and his meat which is no bad wage. Donald McPhail is here, I am staying with him still, he has sixty acres, and Walter Brotherston from Coldstream, one hundred acres.

'The winter here is long. The ice floats in the lake like so many peats, and some the size of a house. The Indians say that Hell is made of snow and ice, and they say that heaven is alive with buffalo. There is buffalo everywhere for eating, they belong to no master. There are no masters here, and no stewards, and no pride. If a man be civil he is respected. I have dined with gentlemen and been asked to say the grace. My – (*She stops dead, astonished.*) my wife –'

They wait for enlightenment, amused, curious.

Liza (*reads*)   'My wife Emily joins with me in her best respects to you. This letter is brought by her father, Mr Monroe, who is going home to Edinburgh owing to his health.'

They wait – surely there's more?

Liza (*reads*)   'Your loving brother, Steenie.'

But surely there's more?

Liza (*reads*)   'PS. Tell John Mackintosh if he comes he need bring no axes, just the clothes for the voyage.'

Liza *stares at the letter, nonplussed, lonely.*

Tottie (*softly*)   Buffalo . . . Buffalo . . .

Maggie   Men!

Sara   But it's a grand letter, Liza, and grand news of Steenie. You must write to the wife, you'll get more crack from his wife.

Jenny (*suddenly, merrily, jigging about*)
Woo'd and married and a'
Kissed and carried awa!

*She and **Tottie** jigging about, trying to get **Liza** to jig/dance also – but **Liza** is still taking in the news of the letter, half-thrilled at the news, at any news, half let-down . . . bewildered . . . at the gaps in the*

news, at the fact that Steenie, now married, belongs to her less. **Tottie**
and **Jenny** *dance around her, jostle, even push her, but she doesn't join
in.*

Tottie, Jenny
And is no the bride well off
That's woo'd and married and a'!

They're all thinking over the news. **Liza** *is silent, holding her letter,
tracing the seal, the writing, with her finger. She pays only intermittent
attention to the ensuing conversation, goes off to some quiet corner to sit
with her letter, or goes offstage.*

Sara   Walter Brotherston! A hundred acres! (*She starts to
laugh.*) Well, he was a young limmer and no mistake!
Remember the night of that kirn at Westlea?

Maggie (*frosty*)   I certainly do.

Sara (*enjoying herself*)   There were half a dozen bairns – the
wee ones, just babies – sleeping in the hay at the farthest end
of the barn. Oh, they were good as gold, not a cheep out of
them, and of course around dawn everyone started for home,
and the mothers were tired out, and the babies sleeping like
the dead. So it wasn't till later, till they were all home, that
they found out what Walter had done!

Maggie   He should have been whipped!

Sara   It wasn't just him, it was Jamie as well. They'd
changed the babies round. They'd changed all the clothes,
the bonnets and shawls. Six babies! – and all of them home
with the wrong mother!

Jenny   But they'd notice, the mothers!

Sara (*laughing*)   Eventually! What a squawking and
screeching across the fields – it sounded like a fox had got
amongst the hens.

Maggie (*muttering under* **Sara**'*s words*)   A swearing scandal,
that's what it was!

Sara   The blacksmith's bairn was away up the hill with the shepherd and his wife! And Maggie's wee Tam ended up in the village, who was he with again, Maggie, was it Phoebe?

Maggie (*grim*)   I went to feed and change my bairn – and he'd turned into a lassie! Oh, you can laugh. But there's many a baby been changed by the Gyptians – so what was I to think? He was never a Christian that Walter Brotherston – and neither's that scoundrel Jamie Dodds. They aye watch him at the kirk! He'll more likely take money out the plate than put anything in.

Jenny   And when he does put something in, it's only a halfpenny.

Sara   There's plenty he gives that no one knows of. He gives to the needy. Many a time.

Maggie (*grudgingly*)   He's a grand worker, I'll grant you that.

Sara   Ay. (. . .) The maister will be keeping *him* on, likely.

A pause. These days they are all nagged by the same thought.

Has he spoken to Andra yet, the maister?

Maggie   No. Not yet. Has he spoken to you?

Sara   No.

Jenny   You don't need to fret, Sara. Ellen said you were biding on.

Sara   Well, he hasn't spoken yet.

Maggie   Maybe he's waiting till he's paid his rents. He'll be paying the rents on Friday – down at the inn. They say the Marquis'll be there to collect in person this year. And the usual grand dinner for the tenants.

Jenny   Hare soup. And goose. And plum pudding. And whisky 'as required'.

They dwell on this in silence. The conversation is becoming desultory, the scene ends (and light fades) quietly, conversationally.

Jenny   The chimneypiece at the inn takes up most of one wall. I've seen it from the yard, I've keeked through the window. They don't need candles with a blaze like yon.

They dwell on this too.

Tottie   Plum pudding. Buffalo.

Jenny   I wish I was a hedgehog . . . or a frog . . .

Tottie   You're a cuckoo!

Jenny   I wish I was. A frog. A cuckoo. I don't know what they do in the winter, those beasts. But you never see them working the fields.

Everyone has left by now, except **Tottie**.

Tottie
Buffalo, buffalo, run up to heaven
For they want you all dead
And you'll soon be all gone.
(*Suddenly boisterous.*) Hey for Sunday at twelve o clock
When all the buffalo jump out the pot!

I can read, I can. I can write, too. I can write a grand letter. 'Dear Kello, What fettle? I am in good fettle, hope this finds you in the same. Did you see me in the glass? I saw you in the glass when the clock struck twelve. I want a clock that strikes twelve. I want to lie down right, not leaning up agin the stack. I want a plaidie on the bed, it canna hurt that way. "Come under my plaidie, the night's going to fa' " '. (*She is maybe almost half-singing the next lines, very softly, very low.*)

Come in frae the cold blast, the drift, and the snaw
Come under my plaidie, and lie down beside me
There's room here, dear lassie, believe me, for twa

Scene Eight

Voices/Chorus. Liza, Maggie, Sara, Jenny, Tottie.
*Couple of days since previous scene. Winter afternoon/evening.
Already dark. Lamps or candles.*

From the beginning of the scene **Tottie** *hears and is aware of the commotion, but keeps separate from it . . . as if, by ignoring it, the commotion might simply disappear.*

As the lights go up, there is a great howl from **Liza**. *Then:*

Liza Sara! Andra! Jenny! Maggie! Davie! Sara! Andra!

(*All this goes fast.*)

Voices
Where's the fire?/What now?
What a racket!/What a clash!
Liza?
Liza!
What's happened?/What's wrong?

Liza
Get the maister – Oh! – God! – Someone – doctor – he's hurt.
He's lying all – he's lying all crooked. Bleeding. Dying.

Voices (*coming in half-way through* **Liza***'s last speech*)
Who's hurt?/What's happening?
Who's hurt?/Lying?/Dying?/Bleeding?
Where is he? Where?
Let her speak.

Liza It's Kello. It's Kello. He's lying all crooked on the stable floor. At the foot of the ladder that leads to his chamber. Bella found him. Bella –

Voices
Bella Menteith!
Bella Menteith?
Huh, well – !
Shush, let her speak!

Liza She shouted on me. She's there with him now. He's –
It's Kello.

Voice(s) Why didn't you run to the house?

Liza There's no one there.

Voice(s) Jenny, run to the house.

Liza   There's no one there.

Voices
It's the day for the rents
They're down at the inn
They're all at the inn
The steward
The maister
But where's the mistress?

Liza   There's no one there.

Voice(s)
Fetch water
Whisky
Lineament
Prayer . . .

A pause. Fearful.

Liza (*quietly*)   There's blood coming out of him. Out of his head.

Sara (*to* **Jenny**, *in fact, but as if to several*)   Fetch the trap. For the doctor. Go on now.

Maggie   Yes. Fetch the trap. Go and harness the mare.

Maggie, Liza, Sara *are now watching 'the others' (i.e.* **Jenny**) *go.* **Liza** *obviously not keen to go back to the stables.* **Tottie** *still ignoring it all.* **Sara** *can't move – neither towards the stables to help, nor towards* **Tottie**, *whom she is acutely aware of.*

Maggie (*going now too*)   I'll follow them on. If you'll mind the bairns. Keep the bairn safe from – (*She means from* **Tottie**.)

Sara   Yes, Maggie.

Maggie (*on her way*)   Lying all crooked! That's rich – for a Gyptian! (*A dart at* **Liza**.) Nothing but trouble!

All this time **Tottie** *has been determinedly trying to ignore the rumpus, trying not to care (and not to be noticed), birling the handles of her hoe or graip to and from one hand to the other, or fiddling, doodling, in some other way.*

Liza (*in shock, really*)   Bella Menteith. I was going to the dairy. She called from the yard, from the stable door.

Sara   Who else was there?

Liza   No one.

Sara   *She* found him?

Liza   He fell. There's blood coming out of him where he fell.

Sara   She saw him fall?

Liza   She found him. I don't know. Kello. He's dying.

Sara   Oh, now, you don't know that. I've seen several given up for dead. Why, my own – (*Breaks off, looks at* **Tottie**; *very softly.*) my own . . .

Liza   Bella Menteith. She's no chicken!

Sara   Are you sure there was no one else there?

Liza   There was no one about. I went to the Big House. There was no one about.

Sara (*she's comforting* **Liza**, *calming her*)   It's the day for the rents. They'll still be at the inn. They'll sit long at the dinner. The Marquis is there . . .

Liza   But Andra, and Tam, and –

Sara   They'll be playing pitch-and-toss at the back of the inn. With the stable boys. There'll be whisky going spare from the tenants' dinner. If the farmers drink, why shouldn't the men?

Liza   But not Kello . . . Kello was here . . . Bella Menteith . . . Maggie thinks . . . I wasn't going to the stables, I was going to the dairy . . .

Sara (*ushering* **Liza** *over to the cradle*)   Go and sit with the bairns, my burdie. Go on now, till Maggie gets back. Look after wee Joe. (*Takes her arm, pats her, soothes her – but it's* **Tottie** *who's on her mind.*) Tottie?

Tottie   No.

Sara   Where have you been?

Tottie   No.

Sara   Where have you been?

Tottie   Nowhere.

Sara   You went to the stable?

Tottie   No.

Sara   Then where have you –

Tottie   NO.

Big and strong, or small and wiry – she's more than a match for **Sara** *when roused, as now – she pushes, or threatens* **Sara**, *and moves away. But she's scared . . . and she doesn't move all that far, stays onstage somewhere.* **Sara** *turns away, but stays onstage somewhere.*

Scene Nine

Maggie *is summoned before the maister. He's trying to piece together what really happened. She is answering his questions. The others are present, also summoned to the maister's 'Inquiry'. There are whisperings before/just as* **Maggie** *speaks – Bella Menteith's name being whispered.*

Maggie   Bella Menteith! Well, she's wrong, Maister Elliott. It wasn't like she said. Tottie wasn't – Tottie wouldn't –

Listens to the maister's questions.

Yes, sir. Well: Liza came screaming, and I ran to the stables, and Kello was lying at the foot of the ladder, and Bella Menteith –

Listens to the maister's questions.

Yes, sir. It was dusk. It was getting on for dark. But there was a light in the stables and another in the chamber. But they were all down at the inn, the men, so why would Kello – ?

Listens to the maister's questions.

No, sir. I never saw Tottie. I saw Bella Menteith. Kneeling over Kello. There was straw in her hair.

Listens to the maister's questions.

Yes, sir, I know that, sir. I know what she says. She said it all to me too, right there in the stables: she said she happened to be passing and she heard an argy-bargy and saw Tottie on the ladder, and that Tottie must have pushed him and that all Tottie said was 'it serves yourself right!'. She said Tottie laughed and laughed up there on the ladder and yelled 'it serves yourself right'. I don't believe her, Maister Elliott. It wasn't like she said.

Listens to the maister.

Yes, sir – I know Tottie deaves all the men – Yes, sir, I know she's always after Kello, but she never wished him harm, sir, she's only a bairn. That night of the kirn – there was blood on her claes. He got off scot-free. She thought she was married –

But the maister cuts her short.

Yes, sir (. . .) Thank *you*, sir.

*She is dismissed, turns away, and her next words are not for the maister, but to herself, or maybe for **Sara**, and the others.*

Bella Menteith! It wasn't like she said. There was straw in her hair.

*As **Maggie** goes, **Sara** is putting on a black shawl, picking up a Bible.*

Children (*or children's voices*)
Doctor, doctor, quick, quick, quick!
The black-eyed ploughman's sick, sick, sick!
Look at the blood coming out of his head!
Doctor, doctor, surely he's – ?

Sara   So he died, and was waked. With pennies on his eyes and salt on his breast . . . Poor Kello. He was daft himself, if the truth be known. But he had that knack – horses, women – they softened at the very sound of his voice. And yet . . . no heart . . . no thought . . . no soul. That's what was wrong. If the truth be known. He wasn't all there. Poor young Kello. He was the one who wasn't all there.

Children (*or their voices. They are running around, playing at ghosties, laughing, enjoying scaring each other*)
Oooooooh! Here's Kello!
Here's a ghostie/Here's a bogle!
Oooooooh! Here's Kello!
Kello's coming to get you!
Tottie's seen a ghostie, Kello's ghostie!
Tottie's a daftie!
No all there!
Here's Tottie – Ooooh!

Shrieks of delighted fear. If they are present, and not just voices, they are flapping cloths – aprons, headhankies? – as they dart for **Tottie**, *then dart away again in fear.* **Tottie** *trying to catch them, or hit at them.*

Hideaway, hideaway!
Hogmanay, Hogmanick!
Hang the baker!
Hang Tottie!
Tottie's going to jaaaail!
Stone walls, iron bars.
They're going to put you awaaay!
Hang the baker ower the stick.
Hang the rope round Tottie's neck.

Tottie *lunges at them. They shriek – and run away. They are hiding somewhere, giggling, whispering, shushing.*

Maggie('s voice) (*insouciant, without serious censure*)   Now then, my burdies, what are you up to? Eh?

Child's voice   Tottie's in a swither!

Scene Ten

Tottie, *two* **Warders**, **Maggie**, **Sara**. **Maggie** *and* **Sara** *are working somewhere, preferably in the field, away from the rest of the action.* **Sara** *knows what is about to happen, but can't bear to be there.*

Tottie, *still upset, relieved the taunting bairns have gone. Approaches the cradle, but warily since nowadays she's not allowed near. She picks up the baby's cane rattle – the old type with a bell inside the cane ball. Plays with it a bit . . . goes on playing with it while she's talking – her story seemingly less important than her concentration on the toy, as children seem, when they're trying to impart something that deeply troubles. She doesn't look at the baby, wrapped in her own world.*

Tottie (*not so maternal to the baby as she used to be*)   I'll tell you a story if you like – it's true . . . He was up there in the chamber. He heard me coming up the ladder. Creepy, crawlie up the ladder. 'We don't need you!' he shouted. 'We don't need you now! Tak your hook, you!' He tried to kick me off the ladder. He hadn't any boots on, but I fell off, he made me fall. Ding! And the ladder fell. Clatter! – Bang! And he fell, Kello, from the top, from the trapdoor . . . dunt!

Two figures in grey cloaks – **Warders** *– are creeping up on her. One of them is holding a blanket, or sheet – or maybe they are holding it between them.*

He wasn't hurt bad – he didn't make a noise. Then she started to scream up there in the chamber. Her! Huh! She couldn't get down – and it served herself right – he was giving her the clock and the dresser and the bed – he was giving her the baby – Whoosh! – I heard. Creepy, crawlie up the ladder –

She breaks off somewhere in the last line as she senses the two behind her, turns round sharply. They have the sheet ready for the capture.

(*Faltering, placating, retreating.*) What fettle? Do you want a story? I'll tell you a story. I'll tell you a story of Jackanory.

They have taken hold of her, one on each side. She is paralysed with fear, so doesn't struggle, at first. They wind the sheet around her.

No!

Sara (*she stops work, she's in pain,* **Tottie**'s *anguish is piercing her*)   Oh, no!

The **Warders** *make a straitjacket of the sheet; in two or three well-practised movements, that take* **Tottie** *by surprise, they have made her their prisoner.*

Tottie   No! No!

The two **Warders** *are hustling* **Tottie** *away.*

Sara *and* **Tottie** *both cry out 'NO' two or three times – not in unison – but we can hardly tell which cries come from whom.*

Maggie (*has been watching* **Sara** *anxiously*)   Sara?

Sara (*flatly, not speaking to* **Maggie**)   No.

Maggie   Sara?

Sara   No.

Maggie (*not directly to* **Sara**. *Even* **Maggie** *realises* **Sara** *is beyond conventional comfort at a time like this*)   You can't keep your eyes in the back of your head. She'll be looked after where she's going. Poor maimed creature. The sheriff was right – she'll be better off there. Lucky it's not the jail. (*Lower.*) Lucky it's not the noose! And you won't have to pay for her keep. The well-off pay, but not the poor. There's a ward for the paupers –

Sara   No!

Maggie   I didn't mean ought. Be sensible, Sara – look at it this –

Sara   I'll pay for my daughter, Patie's daughter. I'll pay.

Ellen *has appeared by now.* **Liza** *also – but not with* **Ellen**.

Sara (*turning to* **Ellen**, *a plea*)   I'll work.

But **Ellen** *doesn't speak.*

Maggie (*to* **Ellen**, *a reminder:*)   It's only ten days till the Hiring. The maister hasn't spoken yet.

Ellen   The maister's out. The Elliotts are out. The lease is up – terminated – out. The great Lord Marquis has had enough: the foreign visitors, the mortgages, the politics. Maister Elliott got above himself, it seems: he supports the six-pound rise, he's standing for parliament. The Marquis is angry, very angry. The lease is up and not to be renewed. There'll be no Speaking at Blacksheils. Not this year. We'll be moving on too. Like the rest of you. (. . .) Will you come with us, Sara? I won't keep Betty Hope on. I'd rather have you.

Sara (*she is still in shock at* **Tottie***'s incarceration*)   But where will you go?

Ellen (*a gesture – where indeed?*)   We'll not get a lease round these parts. The Marquis owns all the farms round here.

Sara (*refusing the offer*)   These fields are my calf-ground.

Ellen (*softly*)   Mine too.

Sara   I've nothing else now.

Ellen *turns away, goes.*

Maggie (*getting back to work again, picking up a bucket to feed or milk the cow*)   It'll be cold for the Hiring. Bound to be. It's been a long winter – and more snow to come! (*Wistfully.*) I'd like a house with the two rooms. Maybe we'll get to Langriggs . . .

Maggie *goes off.*

Sara
She would tell me these stories, she said they were true.
She 'saw' them, she said, on the moor, in the mist.
In a hundred years – more –
We'll be ghosts in the fields,
But we'll cry out in vain,
For there'll be no one there.
Fields without folk.
Machines without horses.
A whole week's harvest
All done in one night,
By the light of great lamps . . .
Not the light of the moon,
They won't wait for the moon . . . no need for the moon . . .

Liza   Sara? . . . We'll maybe both get to the same farm, Sara. If we do – will you teach me to spin?

The Straw Chair

In memory of Anne Kristen who read the play,
and for Anne Lacey who played in it

The Straw Chair was first produced in Edinburgh, in 1988, in a co-production by The Traverse Theatre and Focus Theatre. The cast was as follows.

Rachel	Anne Lacey
Isabel	Sharon Muircroft
Oona	Alyxis Daly
Aneas	Derek Anders

Directed by Jeremy Raison
Designed by Jane Roberts
Music by Anne Wood

Characters

Isabel the Minister's wife, 17 years old, from Edinburgh.

Aneas the Minister, a good deal older than his wife, from Edinburgh.

Rachel the 'uncomfortable' wife of Lord Grange, in her 40s.

Oona a middle-aged or elderly islander (but *not* an old crone). Though mostly speaking in English, also speaks in Gaelic.

Setting

The play is set on the island of St Kilda (always called Hirta by its inhabitants), some summer between 1735 and 1740. One area of the acting space must represent the house (no more than a hut, really) where Aneas and Isabel stay. But this area must not be defined so concretely as to be intrusive during those passages of the play in which it does not figure. Ideally, the 'house area' should be ignored as such when the characters are elsewhere on the island, thereby freeing this space to be treated, if necessary, as part of these outdoor scenes. If possible, the remaining space should include some kind of slope – the rougher-surfaced it can be, and the higher it can rise, the better – to convey the rough and mountainous terrain.

The 'house' contains nothing but the minister's kist (a wooden chest which he will also use as table and sometimes chair – since Hirta had not heard of tables or chairs at this time); a cooking pot; a lamp, of primitive, biblical design, with a wick floating in oil; and a bed. The bed – which is set in the wall of the house, and made of that and that alone, i.e. stone – must be defined well enough for the audience to recognise it when it is referred to, and employed, during the action. It has roughly made wooden doors – or failing that, rough cloth curtains.

Rachel's chair was fashioned for her by one of the islanders. Wood being scarce, the finishing touches were of straw, or, more probably, straw rope. It might even have been made entirely of this. The ballad she sings snatches of in Act I, Scene 4 is an old Scots ballad called 'The Demon Lover'. In Act II, Scene 3 Isabel is quoting from Proverbs, Chapter 10 ('The heart of her husband . . . '). Although Oona speaks mainly English and only a little Gaelic, her Gaelic words, and the Gaelic accent/cadence with which she speaks English, are vital elements of the play.

Hirta is a beautiful place, and was productive in the eighteenth century (compared, that is, with some of the rest of the Western Highlands). The set should not be unrelievedly dreich: there should be something, however slight, about either the sky or the ground – some slight touch, too, perhaps, in the costumes of the women – to relieve the eye of the audience.

(Ideally, there should be two extras [MacLeod's men] to carry on the kist in the opening scene, and to carry it away again in the penultimate scene in Act II when Aneas informs Isabel that they must leave the island. But their inclusion is not absolutely necessary.)

Act One

Scene One

Early evening.
As the lights go up, **Isabel** *is looking around her in mounting dismay. She is clutching a package wrapped in oil cloth – the only extra piece of luggage besides the kist. The kist stands already in the house (unless the cast can include two extras who carry the kist on here; who acknowledge, and are acknowledged by,* **Isabel**, *shyly, with a phrase or two of Gaelic greeting which* **Isabel** *responds to politely but does not understand).*

Isabel *puts down her package, picks up the lamp, and inspects the new, bare home – including the bed in the wall.*

Aneas *enters and goes to the house. He notes* **Isabel**'s *dismay.*

Isabel Is this – the manse?

Aneas They have made this house over to us for the summer.

Isabel (*not impressed*) It looks like the byre.

Aneas It is. It is both. In winter they share their homes with their beasts.

Isabel Well, I'm glad it's summer, then.

Aneas Isabel, it is the best house on the island, and they have spared us one of their cooking pots. They told me so with pride. I don't think they have an abundance of them.

He looks about him. Tries to think of something comforting to say. Fails.

Isabel They have not an abundance of chairs, either, it seems.

Aneas No . . . Well . . . No . . . (*Trying to keep cheerful.*) We had better go and bid farewell to the crew. The Captain wants to sail again before the wind should turn. Otherwise he might be trapped here some time. (*He is waiting for her to move to leave with him.*) Are you coming?

Isabel   Would you mind very much if I didn't? I feel – still at sea. My legs aren't used to land – everything shifts and sways.

Aneas   Captain Martin will be disappointed. You are a great favourite of his. (*A pause. But she says nothing.*) It would be courteous to thank him and say farewell.

Isabel   If I went with you down to the bay now, I might forget myself – and beg the Captain to take me home.

She is near to tears. He doesn't know what to say. They are awkward with each other. He makes a move towards her – but she turns her attention to the kist.

I will look out your books for you.

Aneas *goes.* **Isabel** *opens the kist.* (*It contains everything they have brought with them.*) *She unearths from the bottom of the kist two or three books. Looks around for somewhere to put them, and realises that there is nowhere in this place. She holds the books a moment, and then – not roughly, but hopelessly – lets them drop back into the kist again.*

A bed made of stones! And a chair made of straw! I shouldn't have come here! I should never have come!

Rachel *enters. She is dressed in island dress. But she wears the traditional head-covering draped round her shoulder, an attempt at elegance.*

Isabel, *closing the kist, starts when finally she notices* **Rachel**. *Thinking her an islander,* **Isabel** *prepares to summon up what little Gaelic she has acquired.*

(*Gaelic*)   *Ciamar a tha sibh?* [How do you do.] (*English.*) I am the Minister's wife.

Rachel (*regal and spitting angry with it*)   My chair!

Isabel (*thinking this is Gaelic, and trying to fathom it*)   I – I don't understand.

Rachel   Do you not speak English?

Isabel Why, yes, of course!

Rachel But you don't know what a chair is?

Isabel Why, yes – I am sorry – I didn't –

Rachel You are no better than the rest of them! This is my chair! Oona had no business bringing it here. The woman's a fool! They are all fools here.

Isabel *lost for words.* **Rachel** *picks up the chair.*

It is the only chair in this vile stinking place. And it belongs to me. I am the highest born here!

Exit **Rachel** *with chair. Pause.*

Isabel Dear God. Dear Lord and Father, from whom all blessings flow – who delivered us safe from nights and days of stormy seas – and a drunken crew . . . please deliver me safely back to Edinburgh . . . as speedily as possible. Please let the summer pass more quickly than summer has ever passed before. Let August come soon, *soon* . . . please . . . *please* . . .

Aneas (*off*) Isabel! . . . Isabel!

Isabel (*more dutiful than urgent now*) And . . . please let me be a good wife to the Minister.

The Minister enters. He has one rough wooden stool in his hand. Places it down in triumph.

Aneas There! From the Captain! With his best compliments! I told you he favoured you, Isabel. He sends his deep regrets that you still suffer from the voyage – and bids you farewell. The skiff is on its way back to the ship.

He looks round for the chair. Can't understand its disappearance. Looks at **Isabel** *inquiringly.*

Isabel Someone came and took it away.

Aneas Oh. Who?

Isabel A woman. She spoke English.

Aneas Ah. (*He nods in a puzzled sort of assent.*)

Isabel Apparently it is the only chair on the island.

Aneas   The only one! (*Rather upset.*) And the Minister is not fit for it?

Isabel   She is the highest born here – so she said. (*Bitterly.*) And the rest 'are all fools'!

Aneas   Isabel? . . . My dear . . . It's only for a few months. The Captain will call for us again in August.

She nods.

Or September.

Isabel   September? (*Sharply.*) September?

Aneas   He will return when he can. When the weather and the winds are favourable. It's never easy to make a landing on Hirta. Often impossible.

Isabel (*alarmed*)   And what if the weather is impossible in September? More impossible than August? What then? What do we do then?

Aneas   We have only just arrived, Isabel – it is hardly time to be planning our departure.

Isabel   I wish it were. I wish it were.

Aneas   You are tired. You need to rest.

Isabel (*growing hysterical*)   Rest! Have you seen where we are to sleep? They sleep in tombs here on Hirta. On cold stones! Damp as wells! They are indeed all fools here – or why would they stay?

Aneas   It is not foolishness that brought us here. It is work. God's work.

Isabel (*contrite*)   Yes. I know.

Aneas   It is years since a missionary last came to St Kilda. There is much to be done.

Isabel   I know that, Aneas. I know.

Aneas (*sadly*)   And already you wish yourself back in your uncle's house!

Isabel   I should haved listened to my uncle and my cousins! I should have waited for you in Edinburgh. I thought I could be useful – but what can I do here? I only know two or three phrases in Gaelic – and when we came ashore I heard not one of them. I understood nothing of what they were saying.

Aneas   But they welcomed you! Warmly! They were astonished that the Minister should bring his wife!

Isabel (*not to* **Aneas**, *and he doesn't hear*)   They would be even more astonished if they knew how she wished to be gone!

Aneas   Astonished. And very curious, Isabel!

Isabel (*to* **Aneas**)   I should never have come here. It was stupid of me, stupid!

Aneas   But I mentioned – both to you and your uncle – that the island was – primitive. You looked forward to the adventure!

Isabel   I didn't know any better. I have hardly been out of Edinburgh. I will be nothing but a burden here. I can't even cook for you – not with that! (*She gestures towards the cooking pot.*)

Aneas   Of course you can cook! The fire burns here like any other! They have already given us a great basket of eggs. And another filled with sea-fowl.

Isabel (*hysteria creeping over her*)   I have never cooked sea-fowl. Never in my life!

Aneas   I daresay they cook like any other bird. The woman you spoke of – the one who speaks English? Surely she will help you?

Isabel   I hardly think so!

Aneas   You are tired. And you have been sick the whole voyage. (*Sympathetic, but awkward, helpless.*) Stop crying. Isabel? Stop! You will feel better in the morning.

Awkward together.

Isabel (*trying to calm down obediently*)   Yes. Yes. Of course I will. I'm not myself. And in the morning I will feel better.

Awkwardly, she turns away. And he turns or walks to where he has a view of the shore, and the ship in the bay.

Aneas   They are squaring the topsails already. They were determined to sail before the wind veered. It was threatening to turn when I bade Martin goodbye.

Offstage (down on the shore), a voice is raised, 'leading in' the first line of a Gaelic psalm. Other voices follow.

The light is fading. It will soon be quite dark.

The psalm continues, always a single voice 'leading in' and the others following.

(*Turning to* **Isabel**.) Do you know which psalm that is?

She doesn't turn to face him, still tearful; merely shakes her head.

'God is our refuge and strength, a very present help in trouble. (*Addressing her directly now.*) Therefore will not we fear, though the earth be removed, and though the mountains be carried into the midst of the sea . . . '

Isabel (*trying to smile*)   These mountains are already in the midst of the sea!

Aneas   Come – we will go down to the shore and lead the prayers for Captain Martin and his crew. That they may have a safe voyage south –

He pauses, waiting for her to take his hand. She does so.

– and a safe voyage back again to take us home in August.

They go. Psalm continues as the lights fade, and for a phrase or two after.

Scene Two

The next day. Different part of island.

Rachel *enters, carrying the little straw chair. Puts it down somewhere, sits on it.* **Oona** *appears, carrying a small wooden bowl,* *with porridge in it. As soon as* **Rachel** *catches sight of* **Oona**, *she gets up, moves her chair to another spot, sits on it again.*

Rachel Go away!

Oona God save you, my lady.

Rachel Go away!

Again she gets up, moves – but uncertain now where it is safe to place the chair.

Get off! Get away! Schemer! Thief! This chair is mine!

Oona I know that. (*Holds out the bowl.*) And this is yours also, my lady.

Rachel (*glancing at the bowl without interest*) I don't want your heathen slops. Porridge boiled with gannet flesh! Sweet Christ! . . . I used to take chocolate. In a porcelain bowl. And brandy in the evening . . . As much as I wanted.

Oona *is surreptitiously taking a mouthful of the bowl's contents.* **Rachel** *sees, and pounces on her.*

Throw that away!

She tries to grab the bowl from **Oona**, *who in turn tries to hold on to it, unwilling to waste good food.*

Oona (*in Gaelic*) *Cha tilg. Tha e bruich. Biadh math a th'ann, biadh math.* [No. [I will] not throw. It is cooked. It is good food, good.]

The bowl ends up on the ground.

(*In Gaelic.*) *Abair cosd.* [What a waste.]
(*English.*) A terrible waste, terrible.

Rachel You are a thief, Oona McQueen. You are paid for that food. You are paid for my keep. And I shall tell the Steward. The next time he comes here. I shall tell the visitor – the one who came on the brigantine – the Minister –

Isabel *has entered.* **Rachel** *sees her.*

(*Raising her voice boldly.*) Yes – and the Minister's wife, too!

Isabel (*Gaelic*)   *La math dhuit!* [*dhuibh*, if plural or 'polite']
[Good day to you!]

Oona   *Dia g'ur gleidheadh, a bhana-mhaighstir.*
[God save you, mistress.] (*Gives* **Isabel** *a nod-cum-curtsy and
beams.*) I hope you are well this morning.

Isabel   Yes, thank you.

She looks to **Rachel** – *who has one hand on her chair* – *defiantly ready
to defend her property.*

The Minister asked me to call.

Rachel   To call?

Isabel (*looking to both of them* – *she never treats* **Oona** *as merely a
servant, even when* **Rachel** *is there*)   I am Mistress Seton, the
Minister's wife.

Rachel   To call! (*The phrase evokes memories; she holds herself
less like a wretch and more like a lady.*) How kind! (*Holds out her
hand imperiously, almost as if* **Isabel** *should kiss it.*) Rachel
Erskine of Grange . . . *Lady* Rachel.

Isabel *takes the hand, drops an embarrassed curtsy.*

(*To* **Oona**, *imperiously.*) You may go.

Isabel   Oh, no! Please –

Rachel (*brusquely*)   Go! Go!

Oona *does not scurry. Calmly picks up the bowl and moves further off.*

(*Screaming.*) I said go, get out, go!

Oona *moves further off still, up the slope, and sits, impassive, holding*
Rachel's *breakfast bowl.*

(*To* **Isabel**.) Sit down. Why don't you? They gave me a
servant, but she is only a native.

Rachel *sits in her chair.*

Sit down. Sit down.

Isabel *perches on a bit of rock, or on the ground.*

Did you have a good journey?

Isabel (*automatically*)   Yes, thank you.

A pause.

No I did not. It was not a good journey at all. I was sick the whole time. Very sick. And very glad to reach dry land.

Rachel   You will not be glad for long then!

No answer to this from **Isabel**.

They wouldn't let me get to the boat. I had a message for the Captain. (*Sharply.*) It was not the Steward's ship?

Isabel   No.

Rachel   The Steward is a liar. All that he says is lies. (*Back to the drawing-room manner.*) I have no chocolate to offer you, Mistress . . . ?

Isabel   Seton. Isabel Seton.

Rachel   Nor tea, neither. What necessities did you bring to Hirta?

Isabel   Very little. Some linen, to make bandages with – should they be needed. For I had heard the islanders spend their time climbing the crags. And some bottles of physique. Tar water mostly.

Rachel   Tar water.

Isabel   It is the best Norway tar.

Rachel   Brandy is an excellent physique. What about the brandy?

Isabel   We did not bring any. We only brought the one kist.

A pause.

Rachel   My lord is in Westminster a good deal nowadays. On affairs of state.

Isabel (*taken aback, but rallying as best she can*)   Ah. That is a great distance away – Westminster.

Rachel   I have never had occasion to accompany him there. He lodges in Niddrie Wynd, when he is in Edinburgh. We . . . We lodge there . . . when we are in town.

Isabel   And – have you lodged on St Kilda long, my lady?

Rachel   Long enough. (*Sudden venom.*) Long enough to gladden the heart of Simon Fraser! Do you know the swine?

Isabel (*shocked*)   No.

Rachel   Simon Fraser, Lord Lovat. You'll have heard of him, I daresay?

Isabel   Yes. I have heard of him.

Rachel   And where are you from, Mistress . . . ? (*She has forgotten the name again.*)

Isabel   Seton. Isabel Seton. I am from Edinburgh. And the Minister, too.

Rachel   I saw you arrive, with the Minister. But I was not close to. He seems an old man.

Isabel   He does not.

Rachel   He walks like one.

Isabel   He is not so old.

Rachel   But a deal older than you.

Isabel   I am seventeen.

Rachel (*not directly to* **Isabel***; quietly*)   I was fifteen when I married.

Pause.

Isabel   What brought you to –

Rachel   'A fortunate match'! That's the expression, isn't it? Said with a sneer, always! How did it happen, I wonder?

Isabel *doesn't realise at first that this is a question.*

In your case, I mean? I suppose he debauched you!

Isabel (*very shocked*)   Aneas is a man of God! You are talking of a Minister of the Kirk! . . . (*Remembering* **Rachel***'s* *position*.) My lady! Besides, what girl would marry a man who had – debauched her . . . or even tried to?

Rachel   Then what men would there be left to marry? Besides a few old men of God!

Isabel (*rising, wanting to be away*)   I wonder if I might just speak with your servant before I go? I'd like to ask her –

Rachel   How long are you and the Minister married?

Isabel   Ten days. We set sail from Leith a few hours after the wedding.

Rachel   And you have been seasick ever since?

Isabel   It was a very stormy voyage.

Rachel   And nearly dawn by the time you'd done praying and wailing on the beach! So – you know nothing yet . . . do you? Of debauchery?

Isabel *has no answer to this*.

You are not very pretty.

Isabel (*with dignity*)   No. No one ever thought me so.

Rachel   At seventeen I was *ravissante*. Lady Rachel, the Law Lord's wife! I went to each and every Assembly. The balls. The dinners. The oyster parties. Don't you love to wear a mask and visit the oyster cellars of Edinburgh?

Isabel   I have never been. I've never been anywhere – except here to Hirta!

Rachel   Hirta! You will not like Hirta! The mice grow big as rats here! The sheep charge like buffalo! This is a hellish, stinking isle.

Isabel   We are only here for the summer. (*Fervently*.) We are only here for the summer.

Rachel (*sharply*)   Are you a Jacobite?

Isabel   No.

Rachel   And your bridegroom – the Minister – is he one?

Isabel (*stung*)   No! – Are you?

Rachel (*a look that spits, but she doesn't deign to reply*)   I wanted to get a message to the boat. (*Referring to* **Oona**, *still waiting patiently at a distance.*) *She* forced me back! She is my jailor!

Isabel   She looks after you.

Rachel   The bitch has stolen all my jewels!

Isabel   No, no – I'm sure she wouldn't do that.

Oona *rises. She has recognised the rising tensions in* **Rachel**'s *speech and is slowly taking steps to deal with it.*

Rachel   Jewels ... husbands ... bairns ... Everything I had, I lost! I was on the island of Hesker before this, you know. Alexander MacDonald was laird there, he said he would let me go. I gave him the rings from my ears and my fingers. But – he brought me here instead! He brought me here! ... I was in misery on the Hesker, but I am worse and worse here!

Isabel   You were brought here? Against your will? But who by? Who did this?

Oona (*to* **Rachel**)   Come now, my lady, it is time you came and had something to eat.

Rachel   They were servants of Lovat and McLeod. I knew them by their plaid. I told them I knew them. They opened the door and rushed into the room. I screamed murder –

Oona (*who is by* **Rachel** *now, murmuring in Gaelic*)   *Tha sin gu leoir comhradh. Gu leoir comhradh. Gu leoir comhradh a nis.* [That is enough talking. Enough talking now.] (*English.*) You must eat now, my lady, and then you must sleep.

Rachel (*pushing* **Oona** *away, or moving away from her. To* **Isabel**)   You heard how the Queen of Spain was put in a prison? And the Princess Sobieski sent to a monastery? And the reasons why? Yet they had friends in high places. The Pope not least among them. Who made peace for both these ladies. If friends take pains for me –

She moves towards **Isabel**.

– if some take pains for me –

Isabel *steps back a little.*

– the same relief may happen to me.

Oona   You must not bother the Minister's wife. She has only just arrived. She is just a lass. A young lass.

Rachel (*to* **Isabel**)   They must hope I am dead now. Lovat and MacLeod. Edinburgh believes I am dead now. Edinburgh, husband, bairns. But I am alive.

Again she moves towards **Isabel** *– again* **Isabel** *freezes or retreats.*

You must tell them that. I am still alive.

Oona *is leading her away.* **Rachel** *shrugs her off, turns back – the society hostess once more.*

I pray you, Mistress – ?

Isabel   Seton.

Rachel   Yes. I pray you, make my compliments to the Minister – until we should meet.

Rachel *and* **Oona** *make their way off. One of them is carrying the chair.*

(*Suddenly stopping again. To* **Oona**.) Oona McQueen, you are trying to starve me! You have given me nothing yet to eat!

Oona   There is food to eat, lady.

Isabel *is watching them go – somewhat stunned by this meeting.*

Rachel (*offstage, or nearly so, muttering low – not necessarily distinct*)   You are a liar. Lazy. Sluttish. And a thief.

Aneas *appears – from somewhere up on the slope, if possible.*

Aneas (*calling to* **Isabel**)   God save you, Isabel! (*And then, in Gaelic.*) *Dia g'ur gleidheadh.* [God save you.]

Isabel (*more to herself than to* **Aneas**)   God save us indeed!

Aneas (*he's had an invigorating morning – in his own sober way*)   Though I meet with the same islander ten times in as many minutes, he addresses me each time thus: 'God save you!' I have talked with everyone on the island today! Every man, woman and bairn. Except the men who are on Boreray – they will not be back for a week or more . . . Have you seen Boreray, Isabel?

Still a bit stunned by her meeting with **Rachel**, **Isabel** *has not been attentive to him. She looks up enquiringly, if absently.* **Aneas** *takes her hand, or gestures to her to follow him, and moves further up the slope.*

Look! Look there. That awesome mass of rock which God has flung into the ocean! That is the isle of Boreray!

Isabel (*intrigued, in spite of herself*)   There are men on that? But how do they land?

Aneas   The one who leaps first from the boat to the rocks is claimed a hero. They compose ballads in his honour.

Isabel   But why do they go?

Aneas   They graze sheep there. But also there are geese. Hundreds of thousands of solan geese. Those were goose eggs that they gave us when we arrived.

Isabel (*with feeling*)   They do not taste like any egg I tasted til now.

Aneas   Have you met many of the women?

Isabel   You said you had spoken to everyone.

Aneas   I spoke with them all.

Isabel   But not the Lady Rachel? Wife to some great lord, she says. You have not heard of her?

Aneas   No. What does she do here?

Isabel   She goes mad. And so should I, if I were abducted to this place.

Aneas   Abducted?

Isabel   Ay. They keep her prisoner here.

Aneas (*not too surprised*)   Well, but Isabel, if she is mad –

Isabel (*cutting in*)   She was abducted by MacLeod's men. She told me so. She said she knew them by their plaid.

Aneas   MacLeod is lord of these isles. He is king here. And the Steward is his kinsman.

Isabel   Her family think her dead, Aneas!

Aneas   Isabel – these are not the Lowlands. Things are managed differently in this part of the world.

Isabel   But she was abducted from the Lowlands. She is from Edinburgh, like us. Why – she lodged in Niddrie Wynd! A stone's throw from my uncle's house!

Aneas   If she is mad, you cannot tell the truth of what she says, now can you?

Isabel   She could not invent lodgings in Niddrie Wynd!

Aneas (*who thinks she would*)   Maybe not.

Isabel   Nor abduction!

Aneas   What is her name?

Isabel   Rachel. The Lady Rachel. She frightens me a little. A lot!

Aneas   Hirta must make a gentle Bedlam.

Isabel *looks puzzled.*

If she is mad, she could be shut up now in some dank asylum with fifty other lunatics skirling round about her. Here she has God's fresh air, a church for worship, quiet neighbours, food, and drink.

Isabel (*bitterly*)   You make the place sound like Arcadia!

Aneas   This place! I have never seen such a place!

But **Isabel** *is not listening to him, brooding over Hirta – and its highest born inhabitant.*

... Some of the men took me to the top of Conachair today. To let me see the lie of their world, they said. When you reach the summit and look over – there is nothing! – Nothing! Just a void, fathoms deep, to the ocean below. Birds float below –

like stars. More screech, and flurry, around ... (*He is lost for words.*) ... Never! ... I have never seen such a place!

He is lost in wonder. **Isabel** *lost in thought.*

Isabel   Aneas?

Aneas   Yes.

Isabel   What are they like – the oyster cellars of Edinburgh?

Aneas (*after a pause, perplexed by the change of subject*)   Oyster cellars?

Isabel   Yes. Have you ever been to one? What do people do there?

Aneas   They eat oysters.

Isabel   Then you've been to them?

Aneas   To the public cellars? Certainly not. I have attended private oyster parties. Now and again.

Isabel   What are they like?

Aneas   After the ladies have retired, we smoke our pipes and talk of politics.

Isabel (*exasperated*)   But before the ladies have retired? – What then? Is there music – and dancing?

Aneas   Yes. Some.

Isabel   Just like at the Assemblies? The Assemblies of Edinburgh! My uncle disapproves! Assemblies mean new gowns, petticoats, slippers ... and masks? ... I have never gone abroad in a mask!

Aneas   I hope you never will!

Isabel   Do you dance, Aneas?

Aneas   Your uncle frowns on dancing.

Isabel   But you do not disapprove?

Aneas (*sadly*)   I disapprove for myself. I am not elegant at dancing!

Isabel   I know the reels and the jigs. I am perfectly elegant at those. We practised in the kitchen, Elizabeth and I. But my uncle never knew!

Aneas   No, he never mentioned you could dance. He told me you had learnt to make pastry, and to spin flax into yarn that was fine enough for cambric. And that you were a sweet mother to your younger cousins.

Isabel   I miss the bairns.

Aneas   You will . . . we will have our own – home. Soon.

Isabel   May I go to the Assemblies – when we are back in Edinburgh?

Aneas (*shaking his head*)   There is no need, Isabel. You are a married lady now. You will be dancing soon enough! There are nine couples on Hirta waiting to be joined in matrimony!

Isabel   Nine weddings!

Aneas   No, no – please God – I shall marry them all on the same day!

Isabel   When?

Aneas   We must wait until the Steward comes. He is expected any time now.

Isabel   The Steward! Why?

Aneas   Because these are courteous people, they wish to invite him. And – perhaps – because his boat will bring provisions to enhance the celebrations!

Isabel   Well – I'll not dance with the Steward, that's for sure!

Aneas   You will certainly dance with him – if he should honour you with a request.

Isabel   He keeps that lady prisoner – that Lady Rachel.

Aneas   He is factor here; and I am Minister. And you are the Minister's wife, and will conduct yourself accordingly.

Isabel   But you will speak to him about the lady, the prisoner?

Aneas (*cautiously*)   I may ask him about her.

Isabel   You will get him to release her back to her family?

Aneas   The Society sent me here in a missionary capacity.

Isabel   Then the lady concerns you, surely?

Aneas   Her soul may be my concern. But why she is here – that is none of my business.

Isabel   But – Aneas! – She is –

Aneas   She is MacLeod's business. And the Steward's.

He has distanced himself; and sits down and opens his Bible. **Isabel** *watches him do so, disappointed in him, frustrated. Lights fade.*

Scene Three

Some days later. It is sunny, peaceful. Maybe as lights go up some birds call overhead. **Oona** *is busy, knitting or carding or spinning. (She could not be sewing, it was the men who did all the sewing and tailoring on Hirta.)* **Isabel** *enters.*

Oona   God save you, Mistress Isabel.

Isabel (*Gaelic*)   *Dia g'ur gleidheadh, Una.* [God save you, Oona.] (*She sits near her.*)

Oona   And God be praised that the men are safe back from Boreray.

Isabel   They've killed a great number of geese. They are piled outside the houses like drifts of snow. And the eggs! Baskets of them!

Oona   Oh, they caught many more than that. But the rest they stored on Boreray. Birds and eggs.

Isabel   Oona . . . the eggs that were given to us when we arrived – there must be hundreds in the basket. Far more than we can eat.

Oona   But you will be here all summer long, Mistress. You will eat all those before the summer is over.

Isabel   But they will not keep that long!

Oona   Keep? But you will keep them in the basket!

Isabel   I . . . I've an idea some of them may already be addled.

Oona (*this is a new word*)   Addled?

Isabel   They – they are no longer fresh.

Oona   But you would not be eating your eggs newly laid, surely?

Isabel   How else should we eat them?

Oona   They are better left for a time.

Isabel   How long a time?

Oona (*comfortably*)   A good long time. They taste better that way. Is it not like that in Edinburgh?

Isabel   No.

Oona   No. It is not like that in Skye, either.

Isabel   Skye? You have been to Skye?

Oona   My husband and I went there with Mr Buchan. Mr Buchan was the Minister who came here many years ago. In the time of the last Steward. I was young then. Mistress Buchan taught me the English. She said she could not learn the Gaelic!

Isabel   Our ship put in at Benbecula, but we did not get to Skye.

Oona   It is a wonderful, vast place. And MacLeod is a wonderful lord.

Isabel   You saw him?

Oona   He wears shoes made of leather. Every day. And inside, his castle is covered with cloth. Good woollen cloth, just hanging there from every wall. A terrible waste of cloth!

Isabel   But you liked it there, on Skye?

Oona   It is not like Hirta. (*Pause.*) There was one thing, though, that we liked very much.

Isabel   Only one thing! What could that be? (*Looks down at her own boots.*) The shoes, perhaps? Shoes made of leather?

Oona (*amused*)   Shoes! Now, what use would they be? You cannot climb the rocks in shoes! And if you cannot climb, you catch no birds – and no eggs, neither! We would starve if we had shoes. We would have feet like Mistress Buchan – soft and silly. Soft as the sorrel that grows on Conachair.

Isabel   Then – what could it have been?

Oona   Those plants that grow tall. More beautiful than all the others. Their leaves spread out on wings, and whisper in the wind.

Isabel   Plants? Trees? Do you mean trees?

Oona   Trees. Yes. Trees. The most wonderful thing of all is when there are many trees growing together. If you walk amongst them they bend their wings and catch at you as if to call you back. I was fearful of that. Their spirits talked so sadly.

Isabel   No, Oona – it is only the wind soughing in the branches.

Oona (*ignores this, almost cuts in on it*)   On Hirta our spirits never talk out loud. Almost never. And when they do, watch out!

Isabel   There are no spirits, Oona. There is only one God.

Oona   No spirits in the Lowlands? (*Chagrin for the Lowlanders.*) There are plenty spirits here. You have seen us pour milk on the milking stone each Sabbath? That is for the Gruagach – the spirit – to keep the kye fertile.

Isabel   But God has told us –

Oona No, no, she is a *goddess*, the Gruagach, not a god. She spoke to Donald McCrimmon once. But that was in the time of the last Steward.

Isabel Have you spoken to the Minister of these spirits, Oona?

Oona No, no. The Minister is a clever man. He can make black marks on paper turn into words, and tell us every story in the Bible. He knows about the spirits!

Isabel He's heard of them, I'm sure. But somehow I don't think –

Rachel (*voice off, plaintive, demanding*) Oooona? . . . Oona? Where are you then? Ooooooona!

Oona (*softly*) *Ochan! Ochan!*

Isabel *Ochan!*

They pause, listening for another call. Blessed silence.

Oona Can you turn marks into words, Mistress Isabel?

Isabel It really isn't difficult. I could teach you if you like!

Oona No, no – I could not learn that, not in a hundred thousand years! (*Confidentially.*) The lady tries it sometimes. But she wants for paper, now.

Isabel Why is she here?

Oona (*reasonably*) She is the guest of the Lord MacLeod.

Isabel But she does not wish to be here.

Oona (*philosophical*) We do not wish her to be here, either. But she is like the great Skua. The bird that brings no good. The bird you cannot be rid of.

Rachel *enters, grotesquely, sadly, garbed. She has changed into the gown in which she was carried off from Edinburgh, which, naturally, is much the worse for wear, split and torn, revealing an embarrassing amount of flesh. She maybe sports a shawl/stole around her, or a makeshift fan of seabirds' feathers.*

Rachel Peat! Oona – more peat for the fire!

Oona   God save you, my lady. The peats are by the door. A great many peats.

Isabel   God save you, my lady.

Rachel *acknowledges* **Isabel**'s *greeting with a grunt and a nod. She walks about a bit, wanting to join the other two women, but not quite knowing how to do so without losing dignity. She walks into the house area and looks around.*

Isabel (*calling over to her*)   The Minister will be back presently. He is talking to the men who have just returned from Boreray.

Rachel   Then I'll wait.

Isabel   Please do.

Rachel (*indicating* **Oona**)   I have to keep an eye on her. She would do nothing all day if I let her.

Oona (*shakes her head in unperturbed denial*)   *Ochan, ochan!*

Rachel (*calling over to* **Isabel**, *confidentially*)   I wouldn't sit so close. They stink of gannet. (*She sniffs at herself, anxiously, then rearranges her assortment of rags, assuming air of refinement.*) Puffins in the porridge! Gannets in the gruel! Even the ale they brew tastes of puffin piss!

Oona (*unperturbed, and not directly to anyone*)   Puffins do not piss! Visitors always smell strange to us, too. (*Quickly, politely, to* **Isabel**.) Oh, not you, Mistress – not now. Everyone on Hirta must soon smell of Hirta! Of course they must! (*Pointedly.*) But the ones who smell strongest – are the ones who smell of too much ale. (*To* **Isabel**.) She was thieving my ale. All the ale I brewed last week – it has all gone. She has been asleep the whole of yesterday and the whole of this morning.

Rachel   Liar!

Oona (*still indirect, calm*)   And what she hasn't drunk, she has hidden away.

Rachel (*she is sitting apart from them now, further up the slope. Scratches herself inelegantly*)   I would like to know what has happened to my jewels!

Oona (*who is accused of this thrice weekly*)   She is always talking about jewels!

Rachel (*scratching, examining her rags*)   I need a new petticoat.

Oona   I don't know why she is wearing those Lowland clothes again. (*Again, she is addressing neither of the others directly.*)

Rachel   Because they are all I have, that's why!

Oona   We give her plenty cloth – and linen for her hair.

Although **Rachel** *and* **Oona** *are arguing now (a regular pastime of theirs), it is* **Rachel** *who cuts in on* **Oona**'s *words, and becomes heated.* **Oona** *remains, for the most part, unperturbed.*

Rachel (*to* **Isabel**)   Do you know what they use to keep their rags round them here? Fish hooks! Sweet Jesus!

Oona   Blasphemy is a terrible sin. (*Genuinely upset.*) May God forgive you!

Rachel   Sin? Sin? This isle is full of sin! It is one great God-forsaken sin!

Oona (*stricken*)   That is a terrible blasphemy. Terrible. Hirta is the most beautiful place that God ever made.

Rachel   Hah! And how would you know?

Oona (*to* **Isabel**)   When the birds arrive in the spring, it is the sweetest place in the world.

Isabel   Yes, of course it is! I can see it is, Oona!

Rachel (*to* **Isabel**, *with real venom*)   Hypocrite!

Rachel *moves even further away from the other two.*

Oona (*to no one in particular*)   She is still full of ale.

Rachel   Hypocrites! Jacobites!

Oona (*to* **Isabel**)   And she has more ale hidden away. I know she has.

Rachel   Bridget never grudged me drink. Nor peat for the fire!

Oona (*softly, indirectly*)   The peats are by the door.

Rachel   And Bridget could sing! Not that girning you cry song! Bridget could sing! (*Not singing, but chanting low.*) Binnorie, oh, Binnorie!

Oona (*to* **Isabel**, *as she prepares to go*)   I have work to do. She will have let the fire die. And there is more ale to brew.

Rachel   That's right – go! – Go on! Go on! Useless, thieving, Highland hag! Go to hell – To Hades – To Hirta!

Oona *has gone.* **Isabel** *wants to follow her, but when* **Rachel** *speaks again – although not directly to* **Isabel** – **Isabel** *doesn't quite like just to walk away.*

Bridget never grudged me. As much claret as I wanted. And the brandy. Brandy is the best.

Pause.

Isabel   Who was Bridget?

Rachel (*ignores the question*)   This is not my best gown. But it has still seen better days than your own! (*Adjusting her dress, hair.*) The fool! Does she think I'd call on the Minister dressed in blue kelt and fish hooks?

Isabel   To be quite honest, I think he might prefer – (*Pauses, fearful of offending, or starting another tirade. Takes a comb from her own hair.*) I have a comb here – would you like me to dress your hair?

Rachel *assents, but silently. Comes nearer.* **Isabel** *indicates where she should sit, and starts trying to comb the tangled hair. A silence at first.* **Isabel** *tugs too hard without meaning to.* **Rachel** *is about to protest.*

Isabel (*hastily, soothingly*)   I will try my best not to hurt you, my lady. But if I tug too hard, you will forgive me, won't you?

Rachel (*relaxing under the grooming*)   I had beautiful hair. Lord Grange loved me for my hair, you know . . . Bridget combed it — not the maid — I wouldn't have *her*! Primping at my lord in the glass all the time! (*Burps loudly, or clutches her stomach as if it pains her.*) Gannets! (*Gives her stomach a hearty thump, maybe burps again. Then all is refinement once more.*) God save us — what the food here does to one!

Isabel (*after a pause*)   Who was Bridget, my lady?

Rachel (*relaxed*)   Bridget was my nurse. Bridget was the only friend I ever had. Bridget was my mother.

Isabel (*nonplussed*)   Your mother?

Rachel   She was better than my mother. She was *there*, always. I couldn't sleep at night unless Bridget was there.

Isabel   My little cousin, Elizabeth, is afraid of the dark. She won't sleep alone.

Rachel   Afraid of the dark . . . Afraid to fall asleep . . . but if Bridget was there — and a little drop of brandy . . . (*Abruptly.*) How do I look?

Isabel   I've not done yet. It is still full of tangles.

Rachel   I have no glass to look in. Have you no glass?

Isabel   You must keep still, my lady.

Rachel   That bit there (*She puts her hand to her scalp.*) — Is it mended, that bit?

Isabel   There is a patch where the hair does not grow. Only a patch.

Rachel (*quite quietly; the grooming soothes her*)   That is where Lovat's men dug it out of my skull. They dug out my teeth and the hair from my head. They had six or seven horses. They tied me on a horse behind Peter Fraser, tied me fast with cloth that I mightn't leap off . . .

Isabel (*after a pause, cautiously*)   When? When was this, my lady?

Rachel   In the winter. The winter a distemper raged through the town. The people's faces were all swelled, and their breasts and throats all sore. An influenza, it was called.

Isabel   That was the winter my aunt took ill and died. Six winters ago. You have been here six years.

Rachel   I was on the island of Hesker first. Alexander MacDonald said he would let me go. I gave him my rings. But he brought me here instead!

She is sunk in misery now. **Isabel** *gives up combing. Pitying her, she takes her hand, or kneels down beside her.*

Isabel   But *why* did they do it to you? Why?

Rachel (*venomous*)   Because they are all liars – and I know about the lies!

Isabel   What lies?

Rachel (*getting worked up now*)   Jesuit lies! Jacobite spies!

Isabel   But what spies? Who?

Rachel   The whole clamjamfry! Simon Fraser, Lord Lovat; and Alexander Forster of Carsbonny; and MacLeod of Muiravondale, and Peter Fraser, toad and lackey, and Mar – sweet Mar, my bobbing brother-in-law!

Isabel (*shocked*)   Your brother-in-law? But – did your husband not suspect? His own brother abducted you?

Rachel   My husband is renowed for his virtue. A pious man. Famous for such rigid piety! Do you know (*She has forgotten now which story she was telling.*) there was a barber's boy once . . . (*But she has forgotten how the story goes.*) . . . but I can't remember now. The story's well kent in Edinburgh.

Aneas *has entered. He is not hiding, but his presence is not obvious to the two women.*

Isabel   Do you have children?

Rachel   Four sons. Four daughters.

Isabel   But they must wonder where you are! Oh, but surely they must miss –

Rachel (*each word a venomous hiss!*)   Vipers! All of them!

Isabel *is startled at the extent of the venom.*

I never wanted children. I wanted my lord. When the first was born – a son – Christ, how he wanted sons! – the canny wife was with me two days, three nights! *He* was in London!

Isabel   It is a long way off.

Rachel   I would have given away the son to have the husband back again! Does he think I'm blind? I see the chambermaid swell by the month – so he sends her packing, and tells me I am mad! When I hear he has a woman in London named Lyndsay – he tells his companions I'm a liar and a witch! (*Venom.*) He has women everywhere! He –

Rachel *stops abruptly, seeing* **Aneas**. *He is rigid with righteousness.*

Aneas   Good day to you.

Isabel (*fearfully*)   Lady Rachel – this is my husband, Mr Seton.

Aneas   Your servant, Ma'am.

Rachel   Minister! Delighted! And how is Edinburgh?

Aneas   It does very well.

Rachel   It is some time since I have been there.

A pause.

I was telling your wife of the reasons why.

Aneas   So I gather.

Rachel *is about to speak, but* **Aneas** *prevents her; continues quickly:*

Pray – do not trouble to repeat the reasons, my lady. I'm sure
my wife will impart them to me. And you are – not yourself, it
seems.

Rachel *pathetically discomfited.*

Rachel (*addressing* **Isabel**, *but indirectly and low*)   Such rigid
piety!

Isabel, *discomfited on* **Rachel**'*s behalf, wants* **Aneas** *to make
amends even though she can see how angry he is – angry with her as well
as with* **Rachel**. *She moves nearer him.*

Isabel (*speaks very low, not only her words, but her look, plead with
him for compassion*)   Aneas! . . . Aneas!

An awkward silence. **Aneas** *searching for something to say.*

Aneas   I hope you are well, my lady? The climate here is
rude. Do you keep well?

Rachel   I am not well – but I am not dead, neither! (*Turns
to face him, with a smile, conventions restored.*) Praise be to our
Maker in heaven!

Aneas   You were not in church yesterday. I hope you will
be well enough to worship with us this evening. I hold a
prayer meeting then.

Rachel (*after a pause, almost inaudibly*)   In Gaelic! Huh!

Isabel   Lady Rachel does not speak any Gaelic.

Aneas   I will pray with you in English. Whenever you
wish.

She makes no response.

It must be some time since you recited the creed and the
commandments to a Minister of the Kirk?

No response.

You may worship and pray in God's house, even though you
don't follow all that's said. My wife does not understand the
language yet, either.

No response.

Have you no Bible? I have another with me I can give you, if you wish?

She moves away, up the slope. She had been nervous, excited, at the thought of meeting him, feels foolish now, and bitter.

(*Calling after her.*) Is it true what the islanders tell me? That you never worship with them?

Rachel (*loudly, defiantly*)   I will worship God again when he delivers me from this damned rock!

Isabel *claps her hands to her mouth.*

Aneas   Isabel? Come!

He waits for her to pass before him, and follows her off. But as he goes he stops a moment, undecided, almost contemplating trying to speak further with **Rachel**. **Rachel**, *up above the slope, turns her back on him. He goes.*

As the lights fade, **Rachel** *doesn't move. There is the sound of the Precentor leading in the first phrase of a psalm – each line sung first by the Precentor, then echoed by the congregation. The psalm continues until the lights go up again for the next scene.*

Scene Four

When the singing fades and the lights go up – dimly: it is night, or rather, dawn – **Aneas** *and* **Isabel** *are in the house. She in her white sark, he in his semmit. He is sitting on the bed, lost in thought. She has just taken off her stockings and shoes – is rolling up her stockings.*

Isabel   Tomorrow – or, rather, today, since it is already dawn – I will not wear my stockings – nor my shoes. I think I will leave them off till I get back to Edinburgh. Silly feet! . . . Soft as the sorrel that grows on Conachair! . . . And you, Aneas – will you go on wearing shoes? . . . Aneas?

Aneas   Scales! . . . Scales!

Isabel   Aneas?

Aneas   Did you hear what that young lad said tonight? When I catechised him? (*Incredulous.*) Did you hear what he said about man's creation?

Isabel   I did not follow the Gaelic. (*Yawning, happy the long meeting is over.*) Almost none of it, in fact. So the prayers seemed very long. But I begin to like the singing. The way the voices soar and swell – they are truly reaching up to heaven.

Aneas (*he hasn't heard what Isabel has said. He is shocked by the prayer meeting's revelations; not angry, but saddened*)   The lad told me that God created man covered head to heel – in scales! And that man lost this good covering through sin – and retains scales now only on his fingers and toes!

Isabel   Scales would be a useful covering on Hirta.

Aneas   Isabel! It is a nonsense – a blasphemous lie! And everyone there – every soul on this island – nodded in agreement with him. They all believe this – this . . . !

Isabel   God would not damn them just for – this! – Surely?

Aneas (*shocked at her*)   Isabel! Salvation can only be reached through belief of the truth. Sanctification of the spirit and belief of the truth!

Isabel   My Lady Rachel was not at the kirk tonight. I saw her outside. Hiding in the shadows, watching us all go in. Poor thing.

Aneas   She is no poor thing. She is a godless, mischievous, evil creature. You are not to speak to her again.

Isabel   That is ridiculous.

Aneas   That is an order!

Isabel   Her house is by the well. I cannot avoid her. And besides – I would not. I would not be so cruel.

Aneas   Everything about her is disgusting and ungodly. Her language, her appearance –

Isabel   But that is not her fault – she has no other wardrobe, no comb, no glass. (*Looking around.*) Well – just see how we all live here!

Aneas   The island women dress decently enough.

Isabel   Aneas, she thought to wear her town clothes expressly to meet you! She thought to be seemly!

Aneas   Seemly! She is nothing better than a strumpet! You are not to speak with her, Isabel!

Isabel   But that's what she lacks – someone to speak to. If she is mad, it is only through loneliness, Aneas – and through being so badly used.

Aneas   I mean what I say. Do you hear?

Isabel (*after a mutinous pause*)   You will minister to eighty-odd islanders, and ignore the one soul who needs you?

Aneas   My work is to catechise the natives and lead them to salvation.

Isabel (*not directly to him*)   The islanders will pray and praise till dawn. Whether there is a minister or no. But the Lady Rachel hides in the shadows outside. Afraid.

She looks towards the bed. **Aneas** *has lain down ready for sleep.*

Aneas   Put out the lamp, Isabel. I am weary.

Isabel (*annoyed at his attitude over* **Rachel**)   I would rather leave it burning. (*Pause. She stands with the lamp, defiant – safely defiant, knowing that* **Aneas** *is probably too sleepy to listen.*) If we have to burrow into a hole like puffins to sleep, may we not at least have a light by us? I keep knocking my head and hands against the stone. I am bruised all over. I could do with some scales. Soft ones, like a snake's. (*She is admiring an imaginary covering of scales on her body.*) I could glide over rocks . . . and slither in the sea. Would you love me, dressed in scales? . . . Aneas? Would you hold me closer if we were both created new and innocent with scales? . . . Would you slither in the sea . . . around me . . . with me?

There is a noise. **Rachel** *stumbling, as she enters. Muttering to herself.*

Rachel   Hell! . . . and damnation . . . Damnation and hell! . . . 'Yon is the mountain of hell, he said!' (*Singing.*) Oh, yon is the mountain o hell, he said.

Isabel *goes to investigate.* **Rachel** *is on the slope.*

Rachel (*singing now*)   Oh, whaten a mountain is yon, she said,
Sae dreary wi' frost and snow?
O, yon is the mountain o hell, he said,
Where Rachel Erskine will go.

She notices **Isabel***. Calls to her.*

Come out of there, whoever you are! Come and dance on the mountain! Come and join the assembly! We will hold a fine ball for the fine folks of Edinburgh! You and me!

Isabel   Hush there, my lady! You will wake the Minister – you will wake the whole village!

Rachel (*singing*)   But hold your tongue, my dearest dear.
Let a' your follies a-bee.
I'll show you where the white lilies grow
At the bottom o the sea.

Isabel (*almost cutting in on this*)   Sssssh. Go back to bed. You must not sing so early in the morning. You will frighten all the bairns! You should be asleep, like them.

Rachel (*elegantly*)   I have never been one for sleep. Lord Grange and his young wife were used to dancing till the morn's light.

Isabel   It is the morn's light already.

Rachel (*not so elegantly*)   Carouse, Isabella! Bring out your man and dance a wee!

Isabel (*approaching near her*)   Be quiet! My lady, you must be quiet!

Rachel (*weaving about, dancing; singing loudly*)
But hold your tongue my dearest dear,
Let a your follies a-bee!

Isabel (*riled*)   Haud *your* tongue, will you?

Isabel *would walk back into the house, but* **Rachel**'s *voice grows louder, blackmailing her to stay.*

Rachel   Do you like him? Don't you want him? Do you? (*She grows ever louder.* **Isabel** *fears* **Aneas** *will waken.*) Don't you? Do you?

Isabel   Ssssh.

Rachel   Well? (*Louder again.*) Well?

Isabel   Yes. Yes. Times I think – yes.

Rachel   Then hoist up your semmit and get on with it! Get on with it!

Isabel *turns away.*

So rigidly pious!

Isabel   No! No. But how can I – hoist my semmit – when *he* is talking all the while about the sanctification of the spirit? He is disappointed in me.

Rachel   He hasn't tried you yet!

Isabel   I don't think he likes me. I don't think he wants me.

Rachel (*without too much concern*)   Ask him! Men lie with less conviction when they have no clothes on. (*She looks at* **Isabel** *for a long moment.*) You have not seen him naked?

Isabel *makes no reply.*

Nor any man?

No reply necessary.

Isabella whats-your-face, you have led a sheltered life! (*Not singing now, so much as quoting from the song – mockingly.*)
Till grim, grim grew her countenance
And drumlie grew her e'ee.

Isabel   Ay, drumlie! I haven't minded six of my uncle's bairns for naught! If you don't hold your weesht – I'll – I'll –

Falters, remembering **Rachel**'*s title.*

Rachel   Two weeks married! You should be abed with him now! Sweetly seduced? Deliciously debauched? (*Louder.*) Or roughly ravished!

Isabel   Be quiet! Be quiet! You will wake him!

Rachel   How does a bed of stone and straw for 'a fortunate match'?

Isabel (*to herself*)   Bed? It is more like a well!

Rachel   How does the man – of the cloth – in the bed?

Isabel   The damp grows on the stones thicker than feathers!

Rachel   Ay, but – how does he grow?

Pause for a reply which is not forthcoming.

What are you? – A mouse? What runs in you? Water?

Looking at the subdued and confused **Isabel**, **Rachel** *suddenly – and uncharacteristically – feels pity.*

Ask him! Take him to bed and ask him! Deeve him! Accost him! Stroke him! (*Exasperated by* **Isabel**'*s uncertainty and distress.*) Bite him!

Isabel (*splutters with shocked laughter*)   I could not!

Rachel   You could. (*Looks at her a moment.*) Well – you could pretend to!

Pause.

(*Inconsequentially.*) Did I ever tell you about the time Lord Grange got bit on the bum?

Isabel *splutters with nervous laughter.*

Rachel   Oh, not by me! It was a fox I had. I'd had her since she was a new-born cub. She was curled in the covers at the

bottom of the bed. He sat down there to put on his hose –
and –

They both start to laugh.

That put paid to some wining and wenching! The lordly bum
turned poisonous! He had to hide at home – eat his meals off
the chimneypiece – sleep on his belly. And I told everyone!
Everyone! Everywhere I went! 'Grim, grim grew his
countenance, and drumlie grew his e'ee!' (*Shrieking,
victorious.*) And serve the bastard right!

Oona *appears.*

Oona (*to* **Isabel**)   God save you, mistress. God save you,
my lady.

Rachel (*not pleased to see her*)   What now? What is it now?

Oona   It is morning, my lady.

Rachel   Yes. Thank God!

Oona   I wondered where you were. (*To* **Isabel**.) She will
not sleep in the night.

Rachel   Black, beastly night . . . blotted with dreams!
Bridget never left me in the night.

Oona   It was you left me, my lady. (*To* **Isabel**.) She will
sleep in the day, but never at night. I will get her to bed soon.
(*To* **Rachel**.) Will you eat now?

Oona *moves towards* **Rachel**, *but* **Rachel** *pulls or moves away,
further up the slope.*

Rachel   Bridget gave me brandy for the night. Even when
I was a bairn. Brandy. For the devils in my head. They aren't
like your spirits, Oona – you don't tame devils with a tassie of
milk on a stone! (*To* **Isabel**.) Do you know, they have a god
here that lives in a well!

Oona (*stoutly*)   He cures many illnesses.

Rachel   They leave him presents! Sticks and stones and
bits of old rag! Hah! They are all fools here!

Oona   It is holy water, the water of Tobar Nam Buaidh.

Rachel   A god in the water, and a fairy in every stone! (*Looks up at the sky – sees something in the sky in the distance.*) And a devil – look! – in the sky!

She points out the bird. All three watch it.

Isabel   What bird is that?

Oona   The skua! It came in March. They have not yet been able to catch it.

Oona *is watching it with hate;* **Rachel** *with admiration.*

Isabel   Do you eat it, the skua?

Oona   Eat it? When the men have caught it, we will pluck out its eyes, and sew back its wings, and send it in a drift. So that it dies a slow, slow death.

Isabel *turns from watching the bird to look at* **Oona** *for a moment, surprised by the hate in her voice.*

Oona   It is the imp of hell!

They are watching the bird in the distance.

Isabel   There is something over there – look, there – on the water!

Oona   A sail!

Isabel   A boat!

Oona (*Gaelic*)   *Se 'n Stiubhard a th'ann! Is cinnteach gur e 'n Stiubhard a th'ann!* [It is the Steward! It must be the steward!] (*English.*) The steward is coming. (*Excited in Gaelic.*) *Tha 'n Stiubhard a tighinn!* [The Steward is coming!] (*English.*) We must tell the others. We will need to help the boat in – we will need everyone down on the shore to help.

Isabel (*Gaelic, excited*)   *Tha 'n Stiubhard a tighinn!* [The Steward is coming!]

Oona *rushes off calling in Gaelic.* **Rachel** *has frozen with distaste and anger at mention of the Steward's arrival.* **Isabel** *rushes to the house.*

Isabel (*shouting to him*)   Aneas! The Steward is coming! The Steward is here!

Oona'*s voice off, in Gaelic. Maybe snatches of other Gaelic voices off.* **Aneas** *is slowly wakening.*

Isabel, *about to follow* **Oona**, *remembers to grab her dress. In her excitement she rushes to the doorway/door area of the house before she thinks to put her dress over her semmit. As she is about to do so, she glances up the slope and sees* **Rachel**. **Isabel** *had temporarily forgotten* **Rachel**'*s hatred of the Steward, and her (* **Isabel**'*s) own recently formed opinion of him.*

Isabel (*with a shrug of apology*)   He is here. The Steward. We must help with the boat. (*But she feels a bit of a traitor.*)

Aneas *has raised himself on one elbow – only just awake.*

Rachel (*dignified; venomous; speaking to no one in particular*)   The Steward is a maggoty liar! All that he says is lies!

Blackout.

Act Two

Scene One

*Music. (Jew's harp or fiddle or bagpipes or chanter.) Dance tune.
Occasional voices shouting out during the dance. Music starts clearly
enough (so that the audience has the sense of the tune), but fades to
background as the lights go up.* **Rachel** *in house area – has just
finished, or is finishing, writing her letter. Hurriedly hides away the ink
and extra paper when she hears* **Isabel** *approaching.* **Isabel** *enters
(Hirta costume and barefoot), singing the dance tune to herself,
holding her shawl above her head, dancing the steps she has recently
learned. Moves across to house area. Stops abruptly when she sees*
Rachel *there.*

Isabel   My lady! God save you! I have not see you, since . . .
since the Steward and his party first arrived.

Rachel (*scornfully*)   So – you have been dancing with the
Steward!

Isabel   I have been dancing with my husband. You should
have joined the wedding celebrations, my lady.

Rachel *snorts loudly.*

You would have been welcome.

Rachel   They are jailors, not friends.

Isabel   But weren't you hungry? Oona could not find you
anywhere. Have you fasted all this time?

Rachel   I am not dead yet!

Isabel   The Steward leaves this evening.

Rachel *snorts at mention of the Steward.*

I am warm with all this dancing. The sun has been burning
without a breeze all day.

Rachel   That's not all that makes you burn. I saw you, and the Minister, up behind the cleits, while the rest were all dancing!

Isabel   We went for a walk!

Rachel (*burst of coarse laughter*)   So – you finally learnt to hoist your semmit after all! I thought it was sheep at first – except you made no noise. Not even a 'baaaaaaa'!

Isabel   It was you? It was you! Those stones clattering – that bleeting that never stopped!

Rachel   I would have cheered you on, but the Minister mightn't have liked it.

Isabel (*outraged*)   You – spy! You peeping, prying – You did wrong – you did harm! – do you know that? If it hadn't been for that – all that noise –

Rachel   Baaaaaa!

Isabel   I am not ashamed. It's you who should be shamed. We are man and wife, we are lovers –

Rachel   Rigidly pious raggedy dolls!

Isabel   We are lovers within the sanctity of marriage. So I won't be ashamed.

Rachel   That's more like it. Now you tremble – there's blood in your cheeks. Be like that – next time!

Isabel   I'll be how I please. And so will he! Sometimes this island seems more crowded than the Cowgate!

Rachel (*mocking mood gone, surprised by the spirit of* **Isabel**'s *fury*)   You did well enough . . . considering. It was a clever move, to take him up there. Better than a bed of stone, eh? Mossy and soft.

Isabel (*icily*)   Shall I tell Oona you have returned, my lady?

Rachel (*ignoring this*)   When my Lord chanced along – at my brother's house, a hunting party – he knew exactly what he was about. A man of the world. Bedding was the only art

he cared to practise. Indiscriminately, as it turned out ...
still ... I didn't know that then. Oh, he was a grand lover. A
demon lover. I was fifteen. He carried me off to Edinburgh.
There was none so happy as me! We would lie locked
together, but listening all the while for my brothers' horses.
We knew they'd give chase. We knew they'd be armed.

Isabel (*interest aroused in spite of herself*)   They would have
shot him?

Rachel   They shot him – shot him into matrimony! There
was none so happy as me. (*Triumphantly, to* **Isabel**.) Laid and
laid and laid again! Yes! But – later! ... I was nothing but a
bolster, to fall on in the dark. And later? Later ... a brood
mare to be serviced when he got back from London. A
raggedy doll to be flung down the stair.

A silence.

Remember the honey times, Isabella ... the honey month ...
the honeymoon ...

Falls silent. **Isabel** *anxious to be gone. The music has stopped.*

Isabel   You must excuse me, my lady.

Rachel   No. Don't go! (*Regally.*) I do not excuse you. I
have something to say. Sit down. Why don't you? Sit! (*Looks
about, trying to collect herself. Retrieves the letter.*) A favour. I have
a letter.

Isabel   That is the Minister's paper!

Rachel   No. Mine. My letter.

Isabel   You are writing to your husband?

Rachel   To my kinsman, Charles Tinwald. A solicitor.
Charles, yes ... his name is Charles ...

Isabel   My lady, it will do no good. There is no way to
send –

Rachel   The boat! The boat leaves tonight!

Isabel   The Steward's boat, my lady. He will not take your
letter.

Rachel   They will not let me near the boat. But you may go. They are loading the rents now.

Isabel   I cannot.

Rachel   The oil and the fish and the feathers – they go straight to MacLeod. But the wool is sent further – I have heard Oona say so – to Inverness, and Leith. Hide it in the wool!

Isabel *is shaking her head.*

(*Imperious again.*) I have the right, surely, to send a letter to my cousin. I am guilty of no crime. I loved my husband.

Isabel   I promise you, my lady, when we return to Edinburgh, I – the Minister will speak for you. He is sure to.

Rachel   These are my words – to my kinsman.

Isabel   He will call on your kinsman.

Rachel   The Minister will refuse! And you will forget! Besides, no one will come for me then – not in the winter. Nobody can. By next year I will be mad – or dead – or they will move me somewhere else – back to the Hesker. Who knows where? They did not even give me food on the Hesker. They wanted me dead. I ate seaweed and mussels, and shit from the sheep. They gave me no clothes. Stole my rings. Everything I had I lost. (*On the attack again.*) You have rings on your fingers, all you women down there – singing and dancing – and coupling ahint the cleits! He told me he loved me ere he got me. It is only a letter to a kinsman. See?

*She tries to push it into **Isabel**'s hands. Someone calls to **Oona** (off), in Gaelic. **Oona** replies (off). **Rachel** takes hold of **Isabel**, grips her fiercely.*

Hide it in the wool! The wool goes to Inverness, and sometimes to Leith! Hide it in the wool!

*She exits, as **Oona** enters from the other side. Seeing **Isabel**, **Oona** calls.*

Oona (*Gaelic*)   *Dia g'ur gleidheadh, a Bhana-mhaighstir.* [God save you, mistress.]

Isabel (*Gaelic*) *Dia g'ur gleidheadh.* [God save you.]

Oona I was looking for my lady. Someone said they'd seen her come this way.

Isabel Yes. She was here.

Music starts up again. Another dance – more vigorous and cheerful than the last.

Oona I am afraid she might steal the Steward's whisky. He keeps it well hidden, but all the same . . . she is cunning. If she makes trouble before he leaves, it will be the worse for me.

There are shouts, off, from the dancers and onlookers.

You should be dancing, Mistress Isabel.

Pause. **Isabel** *stands guiltily with the letter.*

Oona It will finish soon, the dancing. And then the boat will leave.

Isabel *is fingering the letter, wondering what to do.*

Ah! You have been writing a letter! To send with the Steward!

Curiously, but courteously, **Oona** *takes the letter from* **Isabel** *and peruses it closely.*

It must be very difficult – to make all those marks. Very difficult!

Isabel You know how you wonder sometimes whether it's right to do something, or not to do it?

Oona (*in full agreement*) Like whether the day is right for fowling or fishing? Sometimes it takes the mod so long to decide, there's not enough time left in the day to do either! So the men eat what we have cooked, and go to their beds.

Isabel No. I mean things you must decide for yourself alone.

Oona Oh. Like when is it right to jump from the boat to the rocks – after this wave has broken, or the next?

Isabel You are a very good person, Oona.

Oona   I hope so. Hirta is a good place. Only the foreigners are sometimes not so good. Oh – I do not mean you, Mistress Isabel. It is time I found out where my lady has got to. My skua!

Oona goes. **Isabel** *fingers the letter nervously. The dance music quickens. Some shouts from the dancers.* **Isabel** *exits, with the letter, in direction of the shore and the boat. The lights fade, and the music, but it doesn't fade away . . . Fades into a different air, a quieter one, for the start of next scene, which takes place later that same evening.*

Scene Two

Later that evening.

The dance music has faded, and faded into a different air – quieter, thinner; someone playing a whistle or chanter, for himself, idly. Most of the islanders have retired or are retiring. **Aneas** *enters,* **Isabel** *a pace or two behind him. They are a bit awkward with each other, conscious of bedtime – and of the bed. The doors of the bed are more or less closed.*

Isabel   It feels almost strange not to be dancing any more. Like a sailor set ashore.

Aneas   You did not dance with the Steward.

Isabel   He did not ask me.

Aneas   He looked for you for the last dance – before they sailed.

Isabel   I was already down by the shore. I was watching them loading the rents.

Aneas   You should have danced with him.

Isabel   I prefer to dance with you. Three days and nights of dancing! My uncle frowns on dancing . . . If I were in his house now, I would light the cruisie lamp and tell stories to the bairns. Stories about their mother. 'What colour was her hair, Izzie?' 'What songs did she sing?' She was a sweet bannock of a woman. She even smelled like a bannock, warm and floury. My fierce uncle, the enemy of dancing, he wept when she died.

Aneas　She was the apple of his eye. Above rubies.

Isabel　Yes. Yes – but ... What was she – how ... when she was young, and – newly wedded ... how was she? With my uncle?

A pause. He is about to reply when she continues.

I was a twig of a lass when my aunt died. A skinny-ma-link. All of a sudden I grew – swelled. I felt silly – big. The bairns laughed at my titties when they hugged me goodnight. I was so filled with loneliness, it could have burst from me in a flood.

Aneas　Isabel –

Isabel　(*her first word just about in unison with his 'Isabel', interrupting*)　Aneas – I'm sorry. Last night, when we walked by the cleits, I –

Aneas　I was too sudden –

Isabel　(*again cutting through his last word*)　No.

Aneas　Too fierce –

Isabel　No, no, no. I was too – silly. I felt we were watched. There was no one – only sheep! But I thought ... and the thought ... I'm sorry ...

Aneas　The day before the feast began, I heard the women singing as I came from the hill. They were preparing the food, outside Marsali's house. It was hot. They were stripped to the waist; kneading, pounding, stooping, turning. They thought they were alone. The men were on the cliffs. I should have passed by. But there was one ... her hair had come loose, it fell against her breasts. The pale cream of her breasts! When the singing ceased, this one, the one that stirred me so, she sang alone. In English. (*A beat. He meets her eyes.*) I love to hear you sing. I longed for you that evening – but the MacCrimmon child fell ill and you nursed her through the night.

Isabel   And the next night the Steward kept you. Drinking till dawn. And last night, by the cleits, I –

He has unpinned her hair. Kisses her breast. They aren't practised or elegant, it is their very awkwardness that is moving. They are by the bed. It is **Isabel** *who opens the bed-doors,* **Aneas** *being occupied with taking off his shirt or jacket, or caressing* **Isabel**'*s hair, shoulders.*

Isabel *gives a small sound of astonishment; stares, shocked, into the bed.* **Aneas** *follows her gaze – appalled.*

A whisky jar falls out of the bed to the floor.

Rachel (*we do not see her yet. Sleepy, muffled, indistinct groan first, then*)   Bridget? Is that Bridget? Where have you been?

Rachel, *or some of her, appears through the bed-doors, dozy-drunk.*

Night. Night again already. God's curse!

Emerges. Collects herself somewhat at the sight of the Minister – quite a sobering sight. Adopts her society tone.

Ah, Minister! I came to call. A courtesy visit. To partake of the whisky the Steward left you. (*Noticing* **Isabel**.) And Isabella! Good evening!

Aneas *puts out his arm in front of* **Isabel**, *forces her to step back a bit from* **Rachel**.

(*To* **Aneas**.) The whisky the Steward left you is not of the best.

He tries to take the jar off her. She shies, expertly avoiding him.

(*To* **Isabel**.) *Déshabillé?* Both? So early? (*Chucks* **Isabel**'*s chin.*)

Isabel (*low but forceful*)   Go! You must go!

Aneas *is speechless with humiliation – and fury.*

Rachel (*disdaining this order*)   I am the high-born here, dearie. You look – quite *séduisante*! Yes. An improvement. (*Reaches out and pinches* **Isabel**'*s cheek, plumps her breasts.*)

Isabel (*teeth clenched*)   Go! Go!

Rachel *is in no hurry to go.* **Isabel** *has to escort, or even steer her out of the house.* **Aneas** *still helpless, furious.*

Rachel (*as she is steered away*)   There's fire in your cheeks! Quench it among the cleits, eh? (*Now she is going. She offers a benediction, beneficent in her booziness.*) Open wide your arms and legs! Remember the honey time, and keep it holy!

Isabel *dares not look at* **Aneas**, *dares not speak to him.*

Aneas   Go to bed, Isabel!

Isabel   She does not mean –

Aneas   Go to bed.

Rachel (*practically offstage*)   Baaaaa!

Isabel *sits on the edge of the bed. He is bitter, humiliated.*

Aneas   'Let us walk by the cleits!' 'There is no one – only sheep!'

Isabel   I didn't know. I didn't know.

Aneas   You confided in – *that!*

Isabel   No. No. No.

Aneas   Made plans. Snickered with that – Pandarus!

Isabel   No. I don't know what that means.

Aneas (*his tone shows he relents at this, but only very slightly*)   Get to sleep.

She is still seated, hunched, on the edge of the bed. He is trying to calm down, gets into bed, but to the back of the bed, and turns away from her, his face to the wall, leaving her still perched on the edge.

Get to sleep!

Sulkily, she lifts her legs into the bed, shuts the bed-doors with an angry bang.

Scene Three

Next morning. **Aneas** *is up and about.* **Isabel** *still in bed.*

Aneas   Isabel, it's time you were up.

Isabel (*still sleepy*)   How is the weather?

Aneas   Cloudy. These mountains make their own clouds.

Isabel   They are not yet gone to Boreray, then.

Aneas   Who?

Isabel   The women – the young ones! They are to go there – when the weather is right. On their own. For a week or two. They go every summer – for the puffins and the eggs. I would so love to go!

Aneas   You have barely sense to keep from the cliff edge here – you would kill yourself on Boreray!

Isabel   I would not!

Aneas   You would drown getting there! You could not jump from the boat to the rocks in heavy seas like they can! Get up, Isabel.

Isabel (*doing so*)   They will take the tinder box, and one of the cooking pots, and sleep in the ruins of some hermit's house that was built years ago.

Aneas   Hundreds of years ago. Before Brendan or Columba. The first missionaries. *They* made these islands Christian while we wallowed still in ignorance.

Isabel   And now? You think it is the other way round now?

Aneas   How could it not be? The psalms and the Commandments – that is all they learn from one missionary to the next. And yet . . . their faith and hope and charity are as steady as the rock they live on. To be missionary here is – a lesson in humility. It is – daunting.

Isabel (*gently*)   You are a good missionary, husband. A very good missionary.

Aneas   When I was asked to preach in Edinburgh, I would polish my sermon till it shone so smoothly, I think now the sense of it was often smoothed away. I measured words, and wrote them, borrowed them from the Book. Here, I must – speak! From my soul! I cannot clutch a parcel of words in my hand. They do not want that. Besides, I cannot write in Gaelic – only speak it . . . indifferently. 'Take no thought how or what ye shall speak,' said the Lord, 'for it shall be given you in that same hour what ye shall speak.' But – oh – the Lord gives it to me so slowly – so painfully!

Isabel   They do not mind if you speak slow. Would you speak like the Steward? Gabbing fast so they could not follow! I watched him do that. He thought himself so grand!

Pause.

Do you remember, before the Steward came – you had been talking to the men, down by the shore. You were talking to them of the crucifixion. Of course, they have heard of it before. But it's years since the Reverend Buchan was here. Maybe they misremembered. Maybe you told it differently, better. That evening I met one of the women – it was Giorsal – on my way to the well. There were tears in her eyes. 'My brothers have just told me the story of the Cross,' she said. And she told it to me – as if I did not yet know it – as if she had just heard the news herself, passing by Gethsemane. 'That he should die for us,' she said. 'Each one of us here on Hirta!' The tears fell into her water pot! So, you see, Minister – you find the right words.

Aneas   I could not find words for you, when I first met you. Each time I called at the house – you had a child on your knee, another at your feet. I was a foreigner. I didn't know the language.

Isabel   They are good bairns, mostly. But they were always so mischievous when you were there.

Aneas   They were jealous. Because I came to see you.

Isabel   You came to see my uncle. On Society business. The Plan to Spread the Gospel in the North.

Aneas Even your uncle did not wish to plan day after day.

This takes a moment to sink in.

Isabel But – you never spoke to me – scarcely seemed to notice me –

Aneas I always loved to look on you.

Isabel I never even combed my hair. Never thought to change my gown.

Aneas You were always bonny. Always more than bonny. But I could not find the words – till I came to Hirta.

Pause. They are looking at each other, last night's anger healed.

I am glad you love Hirta.

Isabel Oh, I do. These women are my friends. The first friends I've had – (*Genuinely.*) Apart from my husband. I have been with no one but the bairns since my poor aunt died. I have been nowhere. Nowhere! (...) I would so like to go to Boreray! It is only for a little while. Aneas – may I not go?

Aneas (*mildly, because there is no question of it*)   Of course not. Your place is here, with me.

Isabel Oona would cook for you while I am gone.

Aneas You have spoken to her?

Isabel Yes.

Aneas You have discussed this with the women?

Isabel Only with Oona.

Aneas *She* put this notion into your head?

Isabel No.

Aneas Who then?

Isabel No one. Why – you! It is you who always climbs up here and gazes out to Boreray!

Aneas (*angry*)   A canny answer, miss! It was the madwoman, wasn't it?

Isabel   My lady? Why, no!

Aneas   The Steward was right – she delights in discord.
Devilment!

Isabel   I have hardly seen my lady. Besides, she would not
talk to me of Boreray. She hates these islands. Her talk is all of
Edinburgh – her family and friends.

Aneas   Your 'lady' has no friends.

Pause. He is very angry now.

Isabel (*the letter is in her mind*)   Well ... I believe she does
have friends, Aneas. (*Guilty, about to confess.*) Aneas. I ought to
tell you this: there is a kinsman of hers called Tinwald. She
wishes to –

Aneas   She has no kinsman – not that would own her. Must
we talk of her again? Yet – since we do – I must tell you that I
have locked the kist. She has already drunk the whisky –
well, no matter. But she must not get my paper, nor my ink.
She has written letters in the past, it seems, and tried to get
them to the mainland. Letters full of lies.

Isabel (*low*)   It is the Steward who lies!

Aneas   The woman has threatened murder, Isabel. She
threatened her husband's life – and that of his family. Why
else would such a man arrange his wife's abduction?

Isabel   He is in league with the Jacobites.

Aneas   For pity's sake, Isabel –

Isabel   Rachel said as much. She is right.

Aneas   He is a pillar of the kirk – a model of piety. A
barber's boy who shaved him once was so moved by his
words that it led to his conversion. The story's famous in the
town.

Isabel   Yet he wishes his own wife dead!

Aneas   Listen to me! I know the devil in all his guises! The
woman is satanic. Even the islanders see that! The skua! And

have you not noticed, whenever we talk of her – a great gulf
grows between us?

Isabel   I would not have a gulf between us.

Aneas (*not accustomed to feeling such rage; controlling it*)   Your
ignorance excuses you. You have never been further than
your uncle's parlour. You have not met her like. (*He thinks
this is an end to it.*)

Isabel   But I cannot walk away from her.

Aneas (*real anger*)   Isabel, she has not fallen among thieves!

Isabel   But she has – they were – thieves and abductors! If
she is wicked, what of Lord Grange – and the Steward . . .
and us?

Aneas (*a pause*)   Your uncle called you douce – but you are
thrawn! Thrawn! There is a lesson you should learn from
your stay on Hirta: the danger of being too troublesome a
wife.

She is bewildered, frightened. He turns to walk away.

Isabel   Then set me on an island – set me down on Boreray!
Forbid me letters from my kin! Tear out my hair!

Aneas   You begin to sound like her!

Isabel (*not shouting; wounded, not just by these words, by his attitude
to* **Rachel**)   You are a hypocrite!

*She had not meant to say so much. Regrets it. But now she has turned
away, can't see this. He wants to speak, moves towards her. But,
thinking herself alone, she moves further off, pulls off her headscarf, and
binds up her hair with it, roughly, tucking in every vestige of hair that
she can, so that as little of it shows as possible.*

(*Low.*) My hair was never bonny! No one ever thought me
bonny anyhow! Hair! Breasts! (*She pulls her shawl or dress
tighter, flattening, hiding her breast.*) Lies!

Aneas *can't cope with this, turns and goes.* **Isabel** *is hunched
miserably, divided between indignation and tears.*

The honey time! Remember the honey time! *What* honey time, my lady? What times? (*Determined not to let the tears flow, muttering to herself.*) . . . 'The heart of her husband doth safely trust in her . . . she will do him good and not evil . . . '

Rachel *enters, with her chair.* **Isabel** *doesn't see.*

. . . 'strengtheneth her arms . . . (*Louder.*) stretcheth out her hand to the poor; yea –'

She sees **Rachel**. *A pause. They look at each other but beyond that don't acknowledge.*

(*Quietly, not for* **Rachel**'*s ears.*) 'She reacheth forth her hands to the needy!'

Rachel (*to* **Isabel**, *calling*)   Hey! Hey!

Isabel (*knows when she is beaten*)   ' – and in her tongue is the law of kindness!'

Rachel (*sets chair down firmly*)   The letter. Was it hidden?

Isabel   Yes.

Rachel   Was it safe?

Isabel   Yes. (*Prepares to go.*) I must go now, Rachel. I have no time to talk.

Rachel   'Rachel'! Well – 'dear heart' – who gave you leave to miss my title? (*Grabs at* **Isabel** *as she tries to pass.*) Hey, hey, hey.

Isabel   I must go. (*But she stops – is stopped by* **Rachel**'*s hand.*)

Rachel   The letter. You hid it in the wool? The Steward mustn't find it.

Isabel   May the Lord and my husband forgive me if he does.

Rachel *doing her utmost to keep* **Isabel** *with her.*

Rachel (*indicating her chair*)   Look at this! All but broken. Oona must mend it. It took her long enough to make in the first place. (*She sits in it; the hostess.*) Sit down, why don't you? Sit!

Isabel *does, with reluctance. A slight pause.*

Rachel   There are no necessities on this hellish rock! No superfluities. I had sheets trimmed with lace, napery of damask. Teapots. Chairs? – Chairs all over the place – you couldn't move but you must sit down! And a feather bed! You would fare better on feathers, Isabel. Though it is the man that counts, not the mattress! The Minister is stickit in more ways than one, eh?

Isabel   The Minister is not stickit, not – in any way.

Rachel   A man his age – and no pulpit to his name!

Isabel   He is a very good Minister. He is secretary of the Society. For the Propagation of Christian Knowledge. Well – secretary to the secretary.

Rachel *is unimpressed. Belches.*

And he is to get a living soon.

Rachel   Soon?

Isabel   After the summer.

Rachel   Where?

Isabel   It isn't yet – he hasn't yet decided.

Rachel   Somewhere as hellish as this, no doubt.

Isabel *is too downhearted to make the effort to get up and leave.*

(*Sharp.*) You did not tell *him* about the letter?

No answer.

The letter! He doesn't know about my letter?

Isabel *shakes her head, without looking up.* **Rachel** *resettles heavily in her chair – daring it to break – sniffs at herself, to check she does not stink.*

Gannets! (*Tentatively, as if in pain, her hand explores her breast.*) I have a pain today. Bad. Those swine! I will see them swing yet!

Isabel *looks up at this.*

(*Starting to laugh.*) I have something else, too, though. Something good! Good! Good!

Goes to some hiding place by some rock, gleefully. **Isabel** *alert, curious.*

Brandy! Brandy! Two gardevins! (*She is holding them up to view.*) The Steward has never had brandy on him before! A present for McLeod himself, no doubt! Losers weepers! Goodbye, Steward! (*Sharp.*) If you tell, I will say I got it from yourself. (*Suddenly, unusually generous.*) Have some!

Isabel *shakes her head.*

Rachel   It is the only thing here that does not taste of fish! It slides down inside, and makes you warm. Like the Minister should have done, when he was in there.

Roughly nudges, or gooses **Isabel**, *who pushes her away – but then, suddenly, vehemently, snatches the bottle from* **Rachel**, *drinks – chokes – drinks again.*

Meanwhile **Oona** *appears with a large jar of water and a bowl of food.*

(*Seeing* **Oona**.) Go away. Shoo! Shoo! Get out of here, go on!

Oona   Food, my lady – God save you! – and God save you also, Mistress Isabel!

Isabel (*guilty, caught with the brandy jar*)   God save you, Oona!

Oona   Food and water. You must eat and drink.

Rachel   I *am* drinking, damn you! (*Imperious, ladylike.*) You may go! Oona What's-your-Face – dismiss yourself – be gone!

Oona (*ignoring the all-familiar reception; turning to* **Isabel**)   You don't look very well, Mistress Isabel. You should make your way back to the village. The Minister is home.

Isabel (*a decision*)   I want to go to Boreray. I will be going with the women. (*To* **Oona**.) Will you cook for the Minister, while I am gone?

Oona   I will be honoured. May you young lassies have calm seas and many puffins! (*Sees* **Rachel***'s brandy jar. Gaelic.*) *Nise, mo Bhean-uasal, de tha seo?* [Now, my lady, what is this?] *O, tha seo eagalach, tha seo direach olc!* [Oh, but this is terrible, this is really very bad!]

Rachel (*after a pause, abruptly, proffering jar*)   Have some.

Oona (*shaking her head*)   We do not drink whisky on Hirta.

An unmistakable burp from the embarrassed **Isabel**.

Rachel   It is not whisky. It is physique!

Oona   It is the Steward's!

Rachel   No, no, no, no. Finders keepers.

Oona   It smells like whisky.

Rachel   Have some!

Oona   My lady (*Proffering bowl and jug.*) – have some of this! It will do you good. Eat!

Rachel (*winningly, suddenly*)   I will eat – if you will drink!

Isael *watches, mesmerised.* **Rachel** *continues at her softest, most beguiling.*

See – Oona – I will put some of it in the jug – with the water. (*Takes jug from* **Oona** *and does so.*)

Oona (*perhaps resisting, but only slightly, as she parts with her water jug. However, she is shaking her head*)   It is the Steward's.

Rachel   Losers weepers. It does not taste of fish. It tastes warm . . . like gold . . . like sunshine on water. Taste . . . I will eat if you will drink. (*Swills the liquid around, hypnotically, in* **Oona***'s jug.*) There – it is mostly water now – holy water from the Gruagach, eh? It will cure the toothache you grizzle over.

She takes **Oona**'s *hand and pours contents of jug into* **Oona**'s *palm.*
Oona *stares, letting it run through her fingers.*

I will eat – if you will drink.

Oona *licks her fingers, tasting.*

No – *taste* it, Oona. Drink it. (*She picks up a handful of food.*) I
will eat nothing if you don't. Isabella likes it well.

Isabel (*guilty*)   I have only had a drop.

Oona *looks to* **Isabel**, *who draws nearer; looks to* **Rachel**, *who
holds the handful of food, ready to eat.* **Oona** *takes a sip from the jug.*
Rachel *crams the food in her mouth.* **Oona**, *wondering, takes a
bigger sip.*

Rachel   You're right. My belly grat for food. So – drink –
just a little more.

Oona *looks as if she might drink again.*

Rachel   It cures all sadness, like the sun.

Oona *drinks.*

Isabel   That's enough.

She takes the jug, to prevent **Oona** *drinking more.* **Rachel** *signals to*
Isabel *to drink, or she,* **Rachel**, *will not eat another mouthful.*

Rachel   It's only a little physique – and a lot of water. Holy
water. Drink, Isabella.

Isabel *drinks.*

(*Laughing.*) Put some fire between your legs! (*She stuffs some
food into her mouth.*) I feel good! Goodbye, Steward! Now he is
gone, I am going to be good, good. Physique makes me so
good. A toast! There is a toast for every glass in Edinburgh!
(*Surveys the other two somewhat wryly.*) 'May never worse be
among us!' (*Drinks. Looks at them persuasively.*) It is a toast!
Drink!

They are lulled by her mildness, pleasantness.

Isabel (*drinks from the jug*)   It is mostly water, after all.
(*Drinks again, passes the jug to* **Oona**.)

Oona (*a sip*) It is warm. And it does not taste of anything like fish. (*Drinks.*)

From now on, **Rachel,** *when she drinks, drinks from one of the jars,* **Oona** *from the jug,* **Isabel** *from either jug or jar. They continue drinking whenever fitting during the rest of the scene.*

Rachel A toast! Another toast! 'May we live for ever – and die happy!'

Isabel (*amused, but puzzled*) May we live for ever!

Oona (*wonderingly*) Well, that is perfectly true. But the Minister tells it the other way round. First you die – and then you are happy for ever. (*Drinks.*) Isn't it? (*Starts to laugh – at herself.*) Now – look at me! Och, listen to me!

They are all laughing.

Isabel (*carried away*) A toast! A toast: to Boreray!

Oona To Boreray! My Finlay lived there for nearly a year. We had only one boat on Hirta. When the storms dashed it to pieces, there were men still on Boreray who could not get home. Fourteen men. They lived there till the spring, till the Steward's boat arrived.

Isabel But what did they eat?

Oona Enough. The cleits are stored with eggs and birds. There is turf for the fire. Sheep for the pot.

Rachel I was a year on the Hesker with nothing! Seaweed and shit! Fourteen men – with a flint – and a cooking pot! Put them on the Hesker, see how they like it!

Oona (*mildly*) They were waiting for the boat, that is all!

Rachel I am waiting! That is all! All!

Pause.

Isabel What will you do if you get – if your kinsman sends for you?

Rachel I will climb aboard and sail to the bosom of my family.

Isabel *gives her a long look.*

Well? Fishface?

Isabel (*greatly daring*)   You have no family – none that would own you.

Rachel   My Lord will do much on the advice of Mr Tinwald. Ought he not to forgive, as he desires forgiveness?

Isabel   Forgive you what?

Rachel   I love him too much, that is my crime. He knows very well. He was my idol. When we were married, there was none so happy as we.

Isabel   The Steward said –

Rachel   The Steward! The Steward and my lord! Peas from the same pod! Hypocrites! Liars!

Isabel   Then – you do not love your husband?

Rachel   I love him too much, that is my crime. He knows very –

Isabel   You threatened him, didn't you? Threatened him with murder?

Rachel   I? I? *He* will be the death of me. We'd been married twenty years ere I came to this. There, he says, there's two hundred pounds a year – pounds Scots! – and a house outside the city walls! Sign! Sign here! He pulled me to the table. My wrist was all but broken. Don't show your face in Niddrie Wynd again. We are no longer man and wife. What God has joined – a document can sunder.

Notices **Oona** *shaking her head, and perhaps muttering in Gaelic.*

What are you shaking your head for, cuddy?

Oona   Man and wife are joined by God. They are joined for ever.

Rachel   True. True. So I went back. Every night. Back to Niddrie Wynd. Shouted. Screamed. Spat at his friends come calling in their carriages. Roll up! Roll up and take oysters with the pious Lord Advocate! See – see what his wife has come to! (*She looks down at her dress, at herself, aware for a moment of herself as she is now.*) ... 'the half-crazed spouse'! ... well ... it takes one to make one. It takes one to know one!

Her rags are coming apart. **Isabel** *goes over to her to adjust what pins/fish-hooks she has.*

Oona   They are terrible, the ways of your world, Mistress Isabel.

Isabel   It is not my world. It is nothing like *my* world!

Oona   Quarrelling like children. To shout like children — when you are grown and married!

Rachel   No one shouts on Hirta? No?

Oona   There is work to be done on Hirta. A woman cannot work if her wrist is nearly broken. A man cannot climb the cliffs and wait for the fulmars to fly in, not if he is shaking ... with hate and sadness. Like you are now, my lady. He would fall. Yes. Surely.

Rachel *sulky. Walks back to her chair, or carries it further off. Then turns on* **Oona**, *suddenly.*

Rachel   You should know! Yours fell! Didn't he? Yours fell!

Oona   *Thuit Fionnlagh! Tha mise ga ionndrain! Tha mi ga ionndrain cho mor an diugh sa bha mi la thuit e. Sheas e air Creag an Leannainna b'fhaide na fleasgach sam bith eile. Sin meud a ghaoil dhomhsa. Bheireadh e ugam buthaidean math agus sheinneadh e orain bhreagha dhomh. An gaisgeach bu chalma. B'fhiach e ceud mile duin' eile!*

(**Oona** *may say some or all of this in English — or all in Gaelic. But the first two phrases should be kept in Gaelic.*) [Finlay fell! I miss him! I miss him as much today as on the day he fell. He stood on the Lover's Crag longer than any other bachelor. That was how much he loved me. He brought me fine puffins and sang me beautiful songs. He was the bravest of the brave. Worth a hundred thousand other men!]

Isabel   Oh, Oona, I am sorry. Don't be sad. *Na bi gul. Na bi gul.* [Don't cry. Don't cry.]

Oona (*crying now*)   *Mo laoch.* [He was my hero.] His spirit is here on Hirta. In some stone or spring. I pray for him every day. When he is released to heaven, then he will be happy for ever. Just as the Minister tells us.

Rachel   God's curse!

The others ignore **Rachel**.

Isabel (*comforting* **Oona**)   Of course he will be happy for ever, Oona. *Na bi gul.* Don't cry.

Rachel (*after a pause; fiddling with her chair; not directly to them; almost sorry about the upset she's caused, but defiant, too, and desirous of attention*)   They all fall in the end! God – what do they expect – trying to live like birds! There are no old men on Hirta!

Oona (*softly*)   He made me beautiful songs, and brought me the finest fulmars!

Rachel (*loudly*)   It's time someone saw to this chair!

She is ignored. **Oona**'s *lament subsided, she wipes away the tears. A pause.*

Isabel   How do you marry on Hirta, Oona?

Oona   How?

Isabel   How do you choose? And when?

Oona   Well . . . a man cannot take a wife till he has a good strong rope.

Isabel *and* **Rachel** *stare at her.*

Rachel (*low*)   Spoken like a Lord Advocate!

Oona (*to* **Isabel**, *noting her surprise; matter of factly*)   The rope is for the fowling.

Isabel   But the bride? Do the parents choose the bride?

Oona (*surprised*)   Why no, of course not – he chooses the one he loves.

Isabel   But what if she says no – the girl? She might say no.

Oona   The man declares his love on the stone. He would not stand on the stone unless he knew she would say yes.

Isabel *is puzzled. She has not heard of the stone.*

Cairistiona hasn't shown you the stone? It is up on the cliffs of Ruaival.

Isabel   A holy place!

Oona (*mildly*)   No. (*Matter of fact, mild – but tipsy, too. The brandy is having quite an effect.*) A dangerous place. A slice of rock, thin as a bairn's arm, a hundred feet above the waves. The man must stand there facing out to sea. On one foot. And hold the other foot in his hands. And look down at the waves. And when he has looked long enough, the other men call him back to the cliff. And the girl says yes.

Isabel *is tipsy enough to find what* **Oona** *is saying funny, as much as amazing.*

Isabel   Those nine men that the Minister just married – they all – ?

Oona *nods.*

There might have been nine funerals!

Oona   No one falls from the Bachelors' Stone. (. . .) I only knew of one.

A pause. But **Rachel** *and* **Isabel** *are curious – their stares force her to continue.*

But he was a foreigner. Poor foolish creature.

The other two still want more of the story. So she obliges.

His ship was sheltering here from a storm. In the time of the last Steward.

Isabel   He loved *you*? He died for you!

Oona (*unhappy about, but not guilty*)   But I never wanted that! I never noticed how he felt. He was just one of the foreigners – with foreign clothes. And a bad foreign smell.

Rachel   Aha!

Oona   I remember he could not eat our eggs. They made him all swollen.

A pause.

Rachel   *That* was what killed him! Unbalanced by his own fart! (*She walks further off.*)

Isabel   I hope you are ashamed, my lady! To say such a thing!

But **Isabel** *is near giggles.* **Rachel** *makes a loud raspberry.* **Isabel** *is giggling now.* **Oona** *shaking her head, but tolerant of them.*

Isabel   You mustn't mock the dead! (*Giggling.*) Oh, dear – I am drunk! Drunk!

Rachel   I would have stood on the stone – once. I was sure of him – then. God – but he could rouse me. There was a tremor in his voice: 'Come here, Rachel – come to me!' Oh!

Isabel *listening, all ears.* **Rachel** *notices – a beat. A change of tone.*

... But the catch was in his voice always, every day. When he called for his broth, or said he was for London. He never took me there. Mouth too loud. No learning.

A beat.

'That Chiesly girl, Rachel! – my dear! You've heard her brothers got her married? To a lord, no less! Fortunate? – a miracle! A vixen! A daftie – like her daddy! The murderer! You know what he said, when he was arrested? "The Chieslys never do things by halves!" Like father, like daughter!'

A pause. For a moment she is aware of what she is – and was. Then sees **Isabel** *is listening, watching, intently. Her own voice again.*

That sack does you no favours, Isabella! Take a look at yourself!

Oona (*the brandy has had its effect*)   Look now – the clouds are lifting. Look now, mistress, look at that sea! So calm! Calm enough for Boreray!

Isabel   To Boreray! (*Drinks.*)

Oona   I wish I was young again. Going to Boreray is better than a feast! No bairns underfoot. No men to feed. No milking in the evenings: just talking and song.

Isabel   The men do not mind when you go there?

Oona   They are pleased when we come back again. Nine months after Boreray – that's when the babies come. You will see, Mistress Isabel – it will be the same for you and the Minister. It will be good for you to go!

Rachel   She'll never get there! And even if she did –

Isabel   Hold your tongue!

They are cutting in, talking on top of each other's phrases.

Rachel   Even if –

Isabel   Hold your weesht!

Rachel   Even if she does –

Isabel   Shut it! Hold it! Shut it!

Rachel (*shouting on, above this*)   Even if she does, she'll not get any bairn from the stickit Minister!

Isabel   He is not! And I will! I will – and he is not!

She grabs hold of **Rachel***'s chair.*

Rachel   My chair! Give me my chair!

Isabel   I'll throw it over the edge if you don't close that gob!

Oona   *A Bhana-mhaighstir Iseabail, na teid an sas 'san fhasgadan!* [Mistress Isabel, do not tangle with the skua!]

Rachel   I'll throw you over first!

Rachel *grabs the chair.* **Isabel** *won't let go.*

So you think you can fight? You?

Isabel   Yes!

Rachel   Go on then!

Each still holding, jabbing, with the chair.

Go on!

Rachel *jabbing and feinting with her end of the chair, fiercely, professionally.* **Isabel** *out of her depth, loosens her hold, lets go.* **Rachel** *falls over, lies still for a moment. Both are still,* **Isabel** *wondering if* **Rachel** *is hurt.* **Rachel** *starts to laugh, lies there laughing.* **Oona,** *who had been watchful, but tipsy, shakes her head tolerantly, now the antics have lost any danger.*

Isabel (*too drunk to be really shocked*)   I am drunk!

Rachel   Ladies are not drunk! Ladies are intoxicated!

Isabel   I am intoxicated.

Oona   *Chaneil feum sam bith a bhi sabaid an fhasgadain!* [No use to fight the skua!]

Rachel   My chair! My poor chair! (*Crawls to the chair, cradles it as if it were a doll.*)

Isabel   I will mend it. I will.

Rachel (*with her chair*)   My Lord Grange has a handsome chair. Muckle great lugs on either side. *His!* No one else to sit in it. A chair to glower in. One time – he was in London – my little vixen got to it. (*Laughs.*) Marked it with her scent. Tore the damask, ripped away the fringe. That's how I found the drawer. A secret drawer on the underside. Opened by a spring. (*Triumphantly, tipsily.*) Stuffed with papers! Letters to my lord! Letters that would send him to Tyburn, or the Grassmarket! To swing! (*Laughs.*) Swing like my daddy-oh!

Isabel   Then he *is* a Jacobite? A spy?

Rachel (*she's staring down in the direction of the bay now. She speaks quietly, almost absently*)   When he parleys with the Jacobites, he is a Jacobite. When he sits in the barber's chair with the burghers ...

Isabel (*tipsy, but trying to work out the sequence of events*)   And when you found the letters – he sent you away? You signed. He paid. Two hundred pounds. Well – so why would he abduct you?

Rachel (*absently; still looking down at the bay*)   Because I would not stay away. I went back every night. (*She turns and smiles at* **Isabel**.) I haunted him!

Isabel *nods agreement with this in tipsy wisdom.*

(*Slyly.*) There are women down there on the shore. They are getting the boat ready! The lassies are off! Without Isabella!

Isabel *rises unsteadily, or moves unsteadily towards viewpoint.*

Rachel (*satisfaction*)   You will never get to Boreray now! Isabella Hum Drum! Isabella Miss the Boat!

Isabel (*on her way, then stumbles. Fear of missing the boat keeps her voice faint. She is hardly more than whispering at first*)   Wait – wait for me! Please!

Rachel   You'll have to leap like a lintie to get down there in time! Here! (*Throws* **Isabel**'s *shawl after her, but* **Isabel** *pays no heed.*)

Isabel (*going, calling out in Gaelic, louder, bolder*)   Fuirich – fuirich rium [Wait – wait for me] Cairistiona – Giorsal – !

Rachel   You'll need your shawl. You'll need it for a blanket! Hey!

Isabel (*offstage*)   Fuirich – O – fuirich! [Wait – Oh – wait!]

Rachel (*watching her go*)   Save your breath for your puffin! It's a long way down! (*Watching.*) You'll never make it! (. . .) By God, but you might! If you don't throw up my physique first! . . . Queer bit of a lass! May never worse be among us! (*Searches for one of the brandy jars.*)

Oona (*happily, dreamily*)   I am spinning in a drift. With the physique. It is like passing into another world. (*A revelation.*) This is what it will be like! Our Father, which art in heaven, I am glad to know this is what the journey will be like!

Rachel (*a toast*)   To Boreray!

Oona   So easy! So soft!

Rachel (*finds the jar or jug is empty*)   God's fart!

Oona   So soft! So easy!

Rachel (*quietly, subdued*)   More ale ... Oona ...

As lights fade, **Rachel** *is rousing* **Oona**, *to help her away down to the village.*

Scene Four

Rachel *is at the kist. She has her chair by her.* **Aneas** *enters. As he crosses to house area,* **Rachel** *beats and flails against the kist, frustrated at not being able to open it.*

Aneas (*hearing these movements as he crosses to the house; eagerly, anxious to make his piece with* **Isabel**)   Isabel?

Then he sees it is **Rachel**. *They stare at each other a moment. Coldly.*

It is locked. There is nothing for you here. Go home!

Rachel (*with a kind of a laugh*)   Home!

Aneas   Oona will be looking for you!

Rachel   Oona is drunk! Drunk as a tink!

Aneas   If that were true – you would find her fit company! I am busy – lady! – excuse me!

He waits, hopes for her to go. Uncertain how to deal with her.

Rachel   You can make peace for me. When you get to Edinburgh. My husband ...

Aneas   You are in my prayers, always.

Rachel   Are you never done praying?

Aneas   I will pray with you now, in English, if you like. (*Suddenly, hopefully, serious.*) Do you wish to pray? Do you wish to repent?

Rachel   I have done no crime.

Aneas   We must all of us repent. Unless ye repent –

Rachel (*interrupting him with an address to the Almighty*)   God – save me from your little ministers!

Aneas (*losing patience*)   Madam, it is no accident you were set on Hirta! It is a remedy! You were an uncomfortable wife –

Rachel   I loved him!

Aneas   Inebriate, violent, dangerous –

Rachel   Loved! Wanted! I would have loved him always. But which mask should I love? He had several – none of them looked on me. Once he got me, he no longer wanted me. When he carried me off to to Edinburgh, we loved – laid – laid again and laid!

Aneas *turns away from her in disgust – wanting to hear no more from her, wanting nothing to do with her.*

. . . But sometimes, even then – the honey time – he'd turn from me as if I wasn't there. Wouldn't speak. So – I'd speak to him – and speak! (*Directly to* **Aneas** *– but as if he is Lord Grange. For the moment, to her, he is Lord Grange.*) Speak to me – speak! (*Strong gesture of frustration – as if wanting to shake* **Aneas**/ *Grange physically – perhaps actually does so.*) Speak, damn you – speak!

Aneas   Calm yourself! You are drunk!

Rachel   Drunk? Yes! Drunk! As a lord! When were *you* ever sober? My sleekit Lord James? (*Still she thinks he is Lord Grange.*) But who would have guessed – save Bridget and me? You never grew warmer with drink inside you. And how could you grow colder than you already were? Whatever you drank, you stayed the same. The same icy, maggoty, biggoty hypocrite! Hoisting skirts in every stableyard, behind every door!

Aneas   This is Mr Seton you talk to – the Minister!

Rachel (*ignores this, doesn't even hear it*)   Bridget's daughter was the only wench you didn't get. Bridget saw to that. But you sent them both away. Who knows where? What happened to Bridget? She was my only friend. Does she live like me now? Or is she already dead? You are capable of anything. You can rid yourself of anyone. Anyone.

A silence. **Aneas** *in shock and trying to absorb what she says – and make out what is true, who are guilty.*

Aneas   I believed it was the Highlands that were sunk in darkness. But there is evil everywhere. Lord, who is blind but thy servant? And I closed my eyes. Kept them shut fast. Only what could I have done? Father in heaven, what would you have me do?

Rachel (*not speaking or looking at* **Aneas** *now*)   Destroy the letters. But Bridget knew. Destroy Bridget. Send Rachel out of town. Tell the world she is half-crazed. But I would not stay away. I haunted Niddrie Wynd. Every night I screamed: murder! Roll up, see the pious Lord of Murder! Oh, I repent! I repent my mouth, my screaming. I should have kept it shut – sought revenge like you seek pleasure – in the dark, in the slime.

Aneas (*his mind is reeling from all this – and its implications on his own behaviour*)   The plan to spread the gospel in the North. I am part of the plan; I was to bring Christ's sweet mercy from the Lowlands. From Edinburgh … where the powerful and the glorious are capable of anything! And rid themselves of anyone.

Rachel (*comes and peers close at him*)   Who's this?

Aneas   Seton. Aneas Seton. Missionary to Hirta. You are on Hirta. Hirta. Go and find Oona! Oona is your keeper!

Rachel (*after a pause*)   It's Isabella's mannikin! The raggedy doll! (*Trying to collect herself, almost conversationally.*) I came for paper. You have paper in the kist.

Aneas   There is nothing for you here. Nothing!

Rachel   Isabella gives me paper.

Aneas   She gives you nothing! Keep away from my wife! Oona is your keeper! And I will say your prayers!

Rachel (*remembering – reviving at the memory*)   No matter. No matter. There is a letter already sent. She hid it in the wool. The wool goes to Inverness. Or even to Leith.

Aneas (*in spite of his state of shock, some of this last speech gets through to him*)   What wool?

Rachel   The rents. Oil, fish, feathers – they go to Skye, to MacLeod. But the wool goes further. The letter will go further.

Aneas   You had no paper. (*But he begins to doubt this.*) You were never let near the boat.

Rachel (*revived, a bit, by mischief: softly spiteful*)   Isabella. Isabella Hum Drum. Hid it in the wool.

Aneas   Lies! *Lies!* (*To* **Rachel** *directly.*) Keep away from my wife! Do you hear?

Rachel   That's easy done, sir! She is gone!

He is too stunned now to react at all. He hears her words but otherwise ignores her presence.

Over the foam. To Boreray. They left before noon. She was the last to the boat, your Isabella. They were already pushed out – they had to lift her from the waves.

She goes – almost offstage – but comes back for her chair. It lies near **Aneas**. *She expects, even hopes, for some aggression, some reaction. But as she retrieves the chair, he does not even notice, sunk in his own despair, fear. So she goes.*

Aneas   Father. Do not punish me with this. Keep Isabel safe. Dear God, keep her safe. Forgive me my sins on Hirta. Do not punish me with this.

Scene Five

Aneas *hurrying onstage, with* **Isabel** *following – she has been told to follow him, he has brought her straight from the boat (which has just returned from Boreray) up to the house. She follows reluctantly. She is caught between the guilt of her disobedient departure for Boreray, and the exhilaration of her adventures there. (She has also come to realise – perversely, in this absence – her affection for* **Aneas**.)

Isabel   But I have still to take my share of the puffins. We have still to divide the catch!

He turns to her, with a look and gesture which usher her firmly into the house.

They are good to eat, puffins. Fresh . . . better than fulmar.

She falters, doesn't realise his silence isn't from anger, and doesn't know how to apologise for going off to Boreray. And so:

We caught thousands, Aneas. We plucked the feathers till our fingers bled. Poor birds. Their beaks bright as rainbows.

Falters again.

Aneas   Oh, Isabel!

Isabel   My Gaelic grows apace! I can sing all their songs. I can laugh with them in Gaelic, even. (*Contritely.*) I led the psalms, night and morning.

A silence.

You won't forgive me. I knew – when I saw you on the shore. The way you looked – wouldn't look – at me.

As he steps near to her, she is quite alarmed, but he holds out his arms, embraces her, caresses her.

Aneas   I thank God to see you safe! Thank God you are safe!

Still embracing her, she responding.

I feared I might lose you.

Isabel   You do forgive me? I thought of you so much. I prayed you would forgive me. But – I so loved being on Boreray! Up on the cliffs – I could have flown! (. . .) Cairistiona was cross. She talked to me of marriage vows. You do forgive me?

Aneas (*his manner shows he does, even though the words do not*)   There is worse than Boreray! You have deceived me twice! Twice over! Isabel – the Steward is here.

Isabel   Yes. We guessed it was his boat. We watched it arriving, from the top of the cliffs.

Aneas   He has found a letter. Cannily hid – in a cleet of wool. One of his men saw you – is almost certain now, now that questions are being asked – that he saw you put it there. Just before the boat sailed. While the rest of us were dancing.

Isabel   I only thought to help her. My lady. I thought I did right.

Aneas   It was right, what you did. Rash, misguided. But right. You have done less wrong than I have. Far less wrong than I have.

Isabel   It will do her no good now, the letter?

Aneas   It will do us great harm.

Isabel   McLeod will get to hear of it?*

Aneas   He's already heard. That's why the Steward is back with his men. Sent by MacLeod.

---

* NB. *If it is possible to have two extras for this scene, it runs thus:*

Isabel   MacLeod will get to hear of it?

Aneas   He's already heard. That's why the Steward is back. Sent by MacLeod.

Isabel   What now? What more can they do? Hasn't she suffered enough?

Two men appear, nod briefly to Minister. **Isabel** *surprised at their appearance.*

(*Addressing them in Gaelic.*) Co sibh? [Who are you?] (*To* **Aneas**.) Who are they? (*To the men.*) De tha sibh 'g iarraidh? De tha sibh a deanamh leis an sin? [What do you want? What are you doing with that?]

Acknowledging her with a slight nod, they have picked up the kist and are carrying it off.

Aneas   MacLeod's men. We are to leave directly. They were only waiting your return from Boreray.

Isabel (*alarmed*)   What will they do? They will make prisoners of us, too?

Isabel (*angry now, not so subdued*)   What now? What more can they do? Hasn't she suffered enough?

Aneas   They have not come for Rachel, they have come for us. We are to leave directly. They were only waiting your return from Boreray.

Isabel (*alarmed*)   What will they do? They will make prisoners of us, too?

Aneas   No. (*Holding her, comforting and being comforted.*) They will set us on the mainland, and send us packing. And you may be sure, our disgrace will reach Edinburgh well before we do.

Isabel   Disgraced! By whom? They will pay no heed in Edinburgh to that parcel of Jacobites!

Aneas   Lord Grange is a government man – or wears the mask of one. A man of power. There will be complaints made to the Society.

Isabel   The Society knows you well. You serve on the committee, they know what you are.

Aneas   They do not know my wife. (*But he had not meant to accuse. Comforts her, tightening his embrace again, or if he is no longer holding her, some gesture.*) Besides – the Society must . . . tread delicately. Its life's work is here – in the Highlands. The Cairistìonas and Oonas and Giorsals of the North. (*Lower.*) While the Granges and Lovats prowl and prosper!

They listened to me, the people of Hirta. Their faith changed me. It made me a priest – which I hardly was before. A bridge to Christ. I saw my life – our life . . . I would have made gardens for the Lord. Not now. I will never get a living now.

Isabel   You will, you will – of course you will.

Aneas   MacLeod's men are waiting. We must go.

He collects some last items – Bible – perhaps **Isabel**'s *shawl.*

Isabel   What will happen now to Rachel?

Aneas   I will speak for her in Edinburgh. I will do what I can. Have you heard her speak of someone named Bridget?

Isabel   Bridget was her only friend.

Aneas (*feels hopeless*)   But the letter has warned them. They will have answers ready. Denials all prepared. Accusations, even. We are small folk, Isabel. The stickit minister –

Isabel   No!

Aneas   And – his beloved wife.

They go.

Scene Six

*Oona is sitting at a distance from **Rachel**, but watching over her. She has **Rachel**'s chair with her, and is repairing it with strands of straw. **Rachel** is sitting. She is 'writing' a letter – the same letter she 'writes'/recites/rehearses constantly. There's no paper, no ink. She has a fistful of quills in her hand. She has shrunk, sunk, since the Setons left. The pain in her breast and the ulcers on her leg have taken their toll. Her leg is wrapped in rough cloth. She has an extra length of wool pinned round her to keep her warm.*

Rachel (*flatly; matter of factly; truthfully*)   Charles Tinwald. Solicitor. Edinburgh. Sir, . . . You cannot know what I suffered since I was stolen. But I must be short. I have a bad pain. And I want for paper.

She looks around, disorientated, chooses one quill from the bunch, examines it absently.

I lodged in Margaret MacLean's house. They rushed into my room, servants of Lovat and Roderick MacLeod, I knew them by their plaid. I cried murder. They dug out my teeth and the hair from my head, I made all the struggle I could. My linens were covered in blood. When we got to Stirling they shut me in a low room, all the windows boarded up, and no light. No light . . . I grew sick, so they let me walk in the court. I gave my rings to the gardener, that he might tell someone I was stolen. But in vain. They put me on a ship.

They were rude and hurt me sore. I was taken to the Hesker.
And then to St Kilda. They are all mad here. I beg you make
haste.

Gingerly her hand explores her breast — she is in pain. **Oona** *stops her*
work a moment, looks up — then continues to thread straw through the
frame of the chair. **Rachel** *rallies a little, adopting her society tone.*

As soon as I am able I will take tea with yourself some
afternoon. I shall have the honour then to wait on you, as I
have of being . . . your servant, Sir . . . and cousin . . . Rachel.

also available

announcing the new Methuen Contemporary Dramatists *series*

Peter Barnes Plays: One
Peter Barnes Plays: Two
Peter Barnes Plays: Three

Sebastian Plays: One

Howard Brenton Plays: One
Howard Brenton Plays: Two

Jim Cartwright Plays: One

Caryl Churchill Plays: One
Caryl Churchill Plays: Two

Sarah Daniels Plays: One
Sarah Daniels Plays: Two

Bernard-Marie Koltès Plays: One

David Mamet Plays: One
David Mamet Plays: Two
David Mamet Plays: Three

Philip Osment Plays: One

Christina Reid Plays: One

Philip Ridley Plays: One

Willy Russell Plays: One

Sam Shepard Plays: One
Sam Shepard Plays: Three

Sue Townsend Plays: One

Methuen Modern Plays

include work by

Jean Anouilh
John Arden
Margaretta D'Arcy
Peter Barnes
Sebastian Barry
Brendan Behan
Edward Bond
Bertolt Brecht
Howard Brenton
Simon Burke
Jim Cartwright
Caryl Churchill
Noël Coward
Sarah Daniels
Nick Dear
Shelagh Delaney
David Edgar
Dario Fo
Michael Frayn
John Godber
Paul Godfrey
David Greig
John Guare
Peter Handke
Jonathan Harvey
Iain Heggie
Declan Hughes
Terry Johnson
Sarah Kane
Charlotte Keatley
Barrie Keeffe
Robert Lepage
Stephen Lowe

Doug Lucie
Martin McDonagh
John McGrath
David Mamet
Patrick Marber
Arthur Miller
Mtwa, Ngema & Simon
Tom Murphy
Phyllis Nagy
Peter Nichols
Joseph O'Connor
Joe Orton
Louise Page
Joe Penhall
Luigi Pirandello
Stephen Poliakoff
Franca Rame
Mark Ravenhill
Philip Ridley
Reginald Rose
David Rudkin
Willy Russell
Jean-Paul Sartre
Sam Shepard
Wole Soyinka
C. P. Taylor
Theatre de Complicite
Theatre Workshop
Sue Townsend
Judy Upton
Timberlake Wertenbaker
Victoria Wood

Printed in the USA
CPSIA information can be obtained
at www.ICGtesting.com
LVHW041056171024
794057LV00001B/112